BEST WISHES™

BEST WISHES™

STORY
MIKE RICHARDSON

SCRIPT, ART, AND LETTERING
PAUL CHADWICK

DARK HORSE BOOKS

EDITORS **CHRIS WARNER AND DIANA SCHUTZ**

DIGITAL ART TECHNICIAN **ADAM PRUETT**

DESIGNER **ETHAN KIMBERLING**

Best Wishes is an original graphic novel, never before published.

Dark Horse Books
A division of Dark Horse Comics, Inc.
10956 SE Main Street
Milwaukie, OR 97222

DarkHorse.com

International Licensing: (503) 905-2377
Comic Shop Locator Service: (888) 266-4226

First edition: November 2017
ISBN 978-1-50670-374-9

10 9 8 7 6 5 4 3 2 1

Printed in China.

Library of Congress Cataloging-in-Publication Data

Names: Richardson, Mike, 1950- author. | Chadwick, Paul (Paul H.), illustrator.
Title: Best wishes / story, Mike Richardson ; script, art, and lettering, Paul Chadwick.
Description: First edition. | Milwaukie, OR : Dark Horse Books, 2017.
Identifiers: LCCN 2017029507 (print) | LCCN 2017030449 (ebook) | ISBN 9781506706269 () | ISBN 9781506703749 (paperback)
Subjects: LCSH: Graphic novels. | BISAC: COMICS & GRAPHIC NOVELS / Fantasy.
Classification: LCC PN6727.R518 (ebook) | LCC PN6727.R518 B47 2017 (print) | DDC 741.5/973--dc23
LC record available at https://lccn.loc.gov/2017029507

IT'S EASIER TO BELIEVE IN *MAGIC* IN THE *OLD WORLD*...
...WHERE STONES HEWN IN *FANCIFUL MYTHOLOGICAL SHAPES*...
...SPILL WATERS THAT SING OF ANOTHER *TIME.*

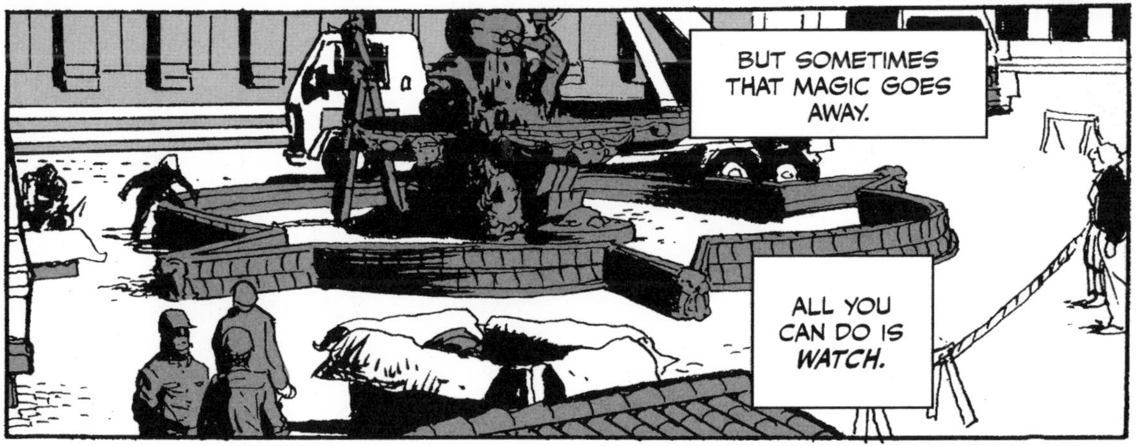
BUT SOMETIMES THAT MAGIC GOES AWAY.
ALL YOU CAN DO IS *WATCH.*

<THEY SHOULDN'T HAVE SOLD IT, MASSIMO.>
<I KNOW, I KNOW.>

<THE TOWN COULD HARDLY REFUSE, THOUGH. THAT'S A LOT OF MONEY. WE NEED IT.>
<IT'S MORE THAN A FOUNTAIN.>
<IT'S THE MOST MAGICAL THING IN THIS PLACE.>

MASSIMO DOES NOT ARGUE WITH HIS WIFE.
HE DOES NOT TELL ROBERTA, "MONEY IS THE MAGIC OF THIS WORLD."
THOUGH THERE WERE TIMES, IN THEIR OWN LIFE TOGETHER, WHEN IT SEEMED ONLY A LITTLE MONEY WORKED WONDERS.
...HAPPY CHILDREN, GOOD HEALTH, AND ACCORD.
THAT COIN, HE REFLECTED...

...WAS THEIR BEST INVESTMENT EVER.

‹ LOOK AT IT THIS WAY, ROBERTA.›
‹ IT GAVE US ITS BLESSINGS IN THIS LIFE. ›
‹ MAYBE IT WILL DO THE SAME FOR OTHERS.›

"< WHERE IS IT GOING AGAIN? >"
"NEW YORK CITY."

NEW YORK HAS MANY PARTS.
THE BROOKLYN BRIDGE...
BROOKLYN...
I REMEMBER WHAT WE TALKED ABOUT, MR. BOLTZMANN...
BUT I THOUGHT I'D JUST RUN THIS BY YOU -- AT NO EXTRA CHARGE.
A BETTER FACE FOR YOUR BUSINESS TO PRESENT.
...WHERE THE SHINING ISLAND OF MANHATTAN...

...CAN SEEM FAR AWAY.
I CLEAR *SEWER LINES.* WHAT KIND OF *FACE* DO I NEED?

CALVIN RUPP
DESIGN ASSOCIATES
GRAPHIC DESIGN
ADVERTISING
SOMETHING THAT SAYS RELIABLE, PROFESSIONAL, YOU WON'T BE GONE IN A YEAR IF THE PROBLEM RETURNS...

WHAT, MY REP ISN'T BASED ON MY GOOD WORD?!
OF COURSE IT IS.

BUT I THINK YOU'D JUST *LIKE* THESE.
FIRST, YOUR ENVELOPES AND STATIONERY...
LOOK.
KID.
BAD SIGN.
I JUST WANT MY SLEAZEBALL EX-PARTNER'S NAME OFF.
THAT SO HARD?
NO.
I'M CALLED TO CLEAR A TOILET DRAINPIPE.
INSTEAD, I TRY TO SELL 'EM A JACUZZI.
THEY GOING TO BE *HAPPY* WITH ME?
NO.

CLEAR...
...THE...
...TOILET.

TIMES ROMAN MEDIUM...

CLICK!

Print

HOW'S THAT?
Ed Boltzmann
Plumbing and Septic
200 Eastern Parkway
Brooklyn NY 11238-605

PERFECT.
I ALMOST HEAR THE WATER FLOWING.
BUT FOR *THIS* I PAY TWELVE HUNDRED BUCKS?

PRETTY GOOD RACKET YOU GOT HERE.
CALL ME WHEN THE PRINTING'S DONE.
WILL DO.

YOU BET I WILL, SINCE I HAVE TO DEPOSIT 30% UP FRONT, IN CASE YOU DON'T PAY THEM.
HOW AM I GOING TO FIND THE CASH?
THIS ISN'T WORKING.
I WAS TOO COCKY.

MR. BRIGGS....CAL RUPP. REMEMBER ME FROM THE SEMINAR YOU DID AT SVA?
WHAT? THAT WAS YEARS AGO!
JUST TWO.
OR THREE.
ANYWAY, YOU SAID TO COME BY WHEN I GRADUATED.
IF I COULD BRING BY MY BOOK--
YEAH, YEAH, DROP IT OFF.

I WAS HOPING I COULD BRIEFLY SEE YOU...
NO. TOO BUSY.

YOU SAID MY PIECE WAS THE STANDOUT OF THE CLASS.
I WAS AN ART DIRECTOR'S CLUB OF NEW YORK SCHOLARSHIP WINNER.
DROP IT OFF.
GOTTAGO. TA.

DORO! THIS STUFF SUCKS!
WE GOTTA REDO IT!

HE'LL NEVER SEE IT.

IT WON'T BE SO BAD, MARY.

BUT JOSH, THIS WAS GOING TO BE *OUR* NIGHT!
FINALLY!
I KNOW, MAR...

...BUT THIS GUY'S BEEN WITH THE TEAM *TWENTY YEARS.*
I *HAVE* TO PUT IN AN APPEARANCE.
C'MON, JUST HALF AN HOUR.

MARY MUSTERS WHAT GRACE SHE CAN.
SHE KNEW WHAT SHE WAS GETTING INTO WHEN SHE STARTED DATING JOSH.
MR. TIEFENWASSER!

HI, WAL.
MARY, THIS IS WALLACE RENFORT, THE TEAM'S PUBLICIST.
WAL, MARY CAPOLAVORO.
MARY.

THE CAMERA'S GOING TO LOVE YOU. THEY'RE SHOOTING A PREGAME FEATURE ON THE RETIRING ASSISTANT COACH.
JOSH, YOU BEAUTIFUL THING!
DO YOU SUPPOSE YOU COULD TAKE OFF YOUR COAT?

YO, ROSIE!
LOVELY GIRL.
THIS WAY, YOU TWO.

ROSIE A FRIEND?
KIND OF.
LATER.
MAKE WAY FOR THE QUARTERBACK AND HIS PRINCESS!
TOYOTA
JUST SAY SOMETHING NICE AND SMILE.
THEY'LL PROBABLY NOT USE A WORD YOU SAY, IS HOW...
EXCUSE US!
...IT USUALLY WORKS.

...WE'RE THRILLED TO BE HERE...
...GREAT GUY WHO HAS REALLY CONTRIBUTED TO THE TEAM'S SUCCESS...
HEY, MAGDA.
YOU'RE HOME EARLY.
JOSH GET TOO FRESH WITH YOU?
I WISH.
NO, A QUICK STOP AT A PARTY TURNED INTO HOURS.
HE CAN'T HELP IT--EVERYBODY LOVES HIM. *I* LOVE HIM.
I JUST WISH HE HAD A LITTLE MORE OF HIMSELF TO SHARE.
WITH ME.
YOU'LL FIND YOUR LEVEL ONCE YOU GET WORK. WITH SO MUCH TIME ON YOUR HANDS YOU OBSESS OVER JOSH.

I'M NOT OBSESSED.
SORRY. BUT YOU'RE DATING A PRO ATHLETE.
YOU HAVE TO BE UNUSUALLY FLEXIBLE.
HOW SO?
NOT MANY OF THEM ARE ONE-WOMAN MEN.

JOSH ISN'T LIKE THAT.
HE'S A MAN, SWEETIE.
WITH INFINITE OPPORTUNITY.

WHAT THE HELL DO YOU KNOW ABOUT IT?!
I'M GOING TO BED!

SLAM!!

...GIFTED THE FOUNTAIN TO THE CITY.
ITS UNVEILING WOULD BE THE PERFECT TIME.

YOU MEAN, TO ANNOUNCE THE NEW CITY SLOGAN AND LOGO?
NO, NO! TO ANNOUNCE THE *CONTEST* FOR THE SYMBOL!
nolan & briggs
SPLISH SPLASH

BUT...I THOUGHT THAT'S WHAT *WE'RE* FOR. N&B HAS MORE AWARDS FOR EXCELLENCE THAN NEW YORK HAS REALTORS!
NO, THE CITY WANTS IT TO BE A CONTEST.
GIVE NEW YORKERS *OWNERSHIP* OF IT.
ANYBODY COULD WIN.

GRAPHIC DESIGN ISN'T A *LOTTERY*...IT'S AN ART! AND YOU'RE AT THE BEST PLACE TO--

...FACILITATE THE CONTEST, AND RAPIDLY SELECT, FORMAT, AND IMPLEMENT THE NEW CITY LOGO AND THEME.
WE'RE EXPERTS AT MAKING A MEME STICK!

THAT'S WHAT WE WANT, MS. NOLAN-- A STICKY MEME!

COUNT TO TWENTY...
GOOD BYE!
...AND HEAR ME OUT.

THIS WILL COVER PAYROLL, RENT, AND DEBT FOR THE REST OF THE YEAR.
AND WHO KNOWS?
JOHN Q. PUBLIC COULD PRODUCE A WORK OF GENIUS.
WE'LL HAVE FIRST CRACK AT HIRING HIM.

...TWENTY!
GAWDDAM THESE WEASEL-SUCKING ASSTACULAR POLITITURDS!!

GLAD YOU SEE IT MY WAY, ROLF.

ALV
ESIGN
GRAPH
RAP RAP RAP

MR. RUPP? YOU IN THERE?

RAP RAP RAP
OKAY, THEN.

CALVIN RUPP
DESIGN ASSOCIATES
GRAPHIC DESIGN

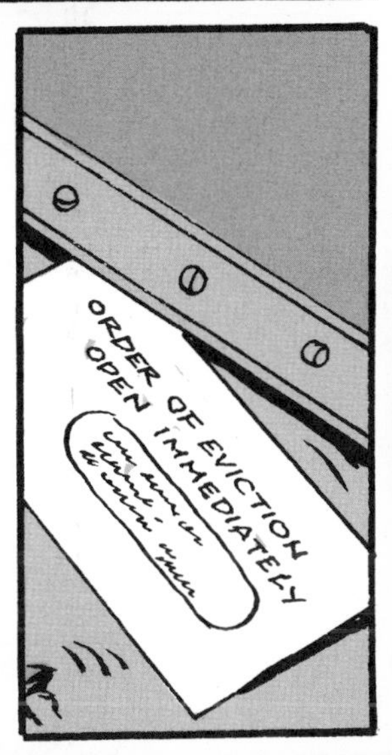
ORDER OF EVICTION
OPEN IMMEDIATELY

TIME WARNER
verizon
NOTICE OF EVICTION
BUSINESS
DOWN DOWN DOWN
Advertising Slump Far From over
SMALL BUSINESS: WORST EVER TIME FOR START
ETRO
CITY

Metro Sectio
The New York Times
The Gift of Pride
ur City"
Erected in Sec
an Old Founta
for Central Park
Unveiling Will Start
Search for New
Symbol for City
By BIANCA MAGIA

HALF HOUR TO GET THERE...
THREE HOURS TO DESIGN...
FIVE MINUTES TO DRESS...
NO, FOUR...

AL, BABE, YOU'LL HAVE TO WAIT.
HEY, TOBY! IT'S CAL RUPP. HOW'RE YOU DOING?
Al's TACO Heaven

BEEN A WHILE, CAL.
WHAT'S UP, BUD? BIG DAY FOR ME TODAY.
NEW YORK CITY HA
SO YOU'LL BE AT THE UNVEILING? GREAT, TOBY!
LOOK, I'VE GOT A BEAUTIFUL PROPOSAL BOOK FOR THE NEW CITY SYMBOL.
SUPPOSE YOU COULD SLIP IT TO THE JUDGES, TOP OF THE STACK, SO TO SPEAK?
YEAH, JUST SO THEY'RE SURE TO CONSIDER IT.
GREAT!
I'LL LOOK FOR YOU ON THE SPEAKER'S STAND WITH THE BIG SHOTS!
NEWS
NEW YORK OUR CITY

THIS IS GOOD, JOSH.

SINCE WE'RE A LITTLE LATE, THE MEDIA WILL BE AT THE SITE, SO IT'LL BE EASIER TO GET YOU THERE.
UH, WALLACE...

I DON'T THINK WE'RE GOING TO DODGE THEM.

MR. TIEFENWASSER!
JOSH!
KISS HER!
OVER HERE!
JOSH!

SURFIN' THE FLESH TSUNAMI, WE CALL IT.
MEET ME THERE, MAR!
YOU'RE GOOD AT YOUR JOB, WALLACE.
WELL, IT DOESN'T TAKE MUCH WITH JOSH.
SOME PEOPLE THE WORLD JUST LOVES.
LIKE MAGIC.

HERE TO HELP CELEBRATE THIS MOMENT, QUARTERBACK FOR THE NEW YORK JETS, JOSHUA TIEFENWASSER!
OKAY, CAL.
TOBY! HEY! HERE IT IS!
HELLO, ALL.
BUT I'M WITH JOSH!
SORRY, MISS, BUT THERE'S JUST NO MORE ROOM.
YOU CAN REJOIN HIM AFTER THE SPEECHES!
CIVIC PRIDE IS LIKE OXYGEN, OR WATER...
...CRUCIAL FOR LIFE...

TOBY--NO!

IN MY TOWN, COVALI, A LEGEND GREW. COINS ACCOMPANIED BY WISHES OF THE DESERVING...
PICK IT UP! C'MON!!

...WILL LEAD TO LOVE AND SUCCESS...

...AND I BELIEVE HERE, IN MY HEART, THAT IT WILL BE THE SAME IN ITS NEW HOME...NEW YORK CITY!

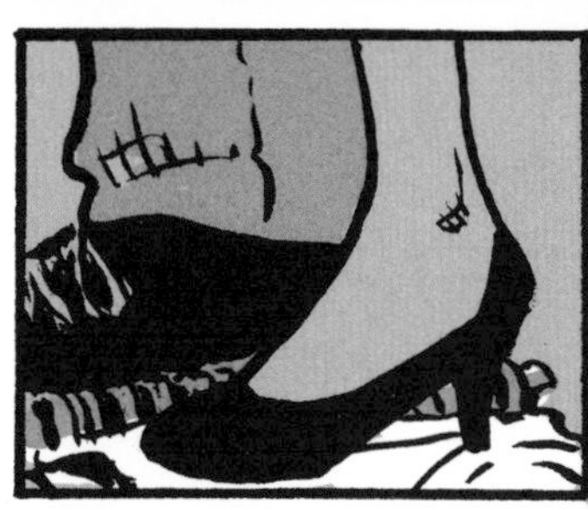

JOSH!
JOSH!

WATER FALLS.

PARK ROUTINE RESUMES.
SODAS

RECENT WORDS, SPOKEN WITH AN ITALIAN ACCENT, ECHO.
WHY NOT?

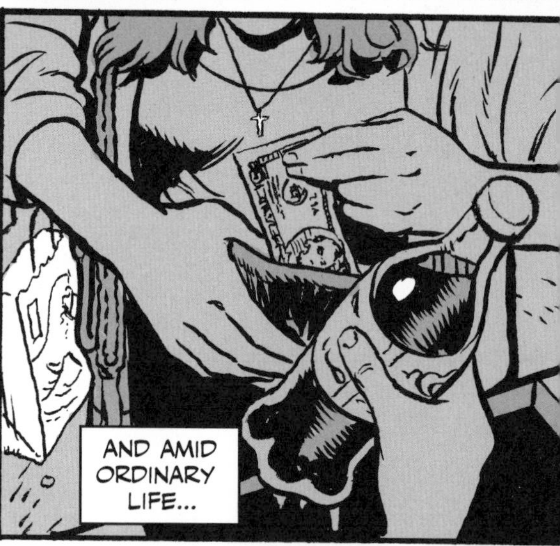
AND AMID ORDINARY LIFE...

...SOMETHING EXTRORDINARY BEGINS TO TAKE SHAPE...
...THOUGH IT, LIKE MANY THINGS, WILL AT FIRST GO UNNOTICED.

HOT D
PRETZ

I WISH...
I WISH...
...THAT THIS TOWN WOULD REALIZE WHAT A TALENTED ARTIST I AM.
...THAT JOSH WOULD LEARN THE MEANING OF TRUE LOVE.

NEW YORK

macy's

?

WHA--?!
macy's

THIS ISN'T MY BAG!

WHO'S GOT MY BAG?!
LIBERTY
IN GOD WE TRUST
QUARTER DOLLAR
E PLURIBUS UNUM

Can this relationship
be saved?
Josh
-Star Quarter-
back
-Gorgeous
-Confident,
popular
-75%?
Mary
ex-ice cream girl
" waitress
" intern
Daddy's
-current job
seeker
OK, if no
chocolate-induced
acne
Resents attention
he gets?
-110% in

ONE "CHOCOLATE DELIGHT."
MORE COFFEE?
NO, THANKS.

MMMM, SINFUL!

MAGDA!
DON'T LOOK SO GUILTY.
I WAS GOING TO ASK YOU TO SHARE!

AND TO LET ME PICK UP THE CHECK.
I OWE YOU -- ME AND MY SMART MOUTH.

IT'S OKAY. I WAS TIRED AND CRANKY.

WELL, I REALLY DON'T THINK YOU'RE OBSESSED WITH JOSH.
WHAT'S THAT YOU'RE WRITING?

OH, JOB HUNTING IDEAS.
TELL ME!

THEY NEED TO PERCOLATE.
I UNDER-STAND.

YOU'VE HAD TROUBLE FINDING YOUR PATH, BUT ONCE YOU DO, LOOK OUT WORLD!
YOU'RE SO TALENTED!

I MEAN, LOOK AT THAT!
IT'S BEAUTIFUL!

MY GOD! THAT'S FANTASTIC!

OH! SORRY!

LUNCH WITH FAT CATS AND THE POLITICIANS THEY OWN...
...IT'S FINALLY OVER.
C'MON, YOU GOT TO MEET JOSH TIEFENWASSER!
OH, JOY.
EVERY WOMAN THERE WAS ALMOST AUDIBLY *OVULATING.*

NOT ME.
THE PRE-MENSTRUAL ONES, I MEAN.
WHAT A DEAR YOU ARE.
HEY, MAYBE THAT SHOULD BE IT. IT'S BETTER THAN MOST OF THE EARLY ENTRIES.

IT ONLY OFFICIALLY STARTED TODAY.
I KNOW, BUT THE EARLY ENTRIES TELL US WHAT'S COMING.
A MOUNTAIN OF CRAP.
TAXI

I STILL SAY WE SHOULD JUST DESIGN SOMETHING IN-HOUSE AND USE A FREELANCER AS A RINGER.
VIN DESTEFANO WOULD DO IT.
VIN, YES...

...WHO CO-OWNS THAT SAILBOAT WITH YOU, I BELIEVE.
AND AFTER HE BANKS HIS PRIZE MONEY, HE JUST MIGHT PICK UP ALL YOUR MOORAGE AND LICENSE FEES...
HEY!
HE'S A PAL, OKAY? SO?

SO YOU COULD GO TO *JAIL* FOR THAT, ROLF.
EVEN IN NEW YORK.
NO, WE DO THIS STRAIGHT.
SOMETHING GOOD WILL TURN UP.

DRIVER, WHY AREN'T WE MOVING?
SOMETHING HAPPENING AT THIS CAFE.
PEOPLE ARE LEAVING THEIR CARS.

DOESN'T LOOK VIOLENT...
TAXI
LET'S SEE.

HEY, WATCH IT, PAL!
SORRY.

ALL RIGHT. WHY THE FUSS?
WHAT, YOU JUST DO THIS?
SHE SURE DID!

WELL, NAIL MY TONGUE TO A TREE AND CALL ME TASTELESS...
...BUT THAT'S IT!

I CAN SEE THIS WORKING EVERYWHERE.
New York Our City
NYOC

TWO MONTHS AND THE CONTEST IS OFFICIALLY OVER.
NOLAN & BRIGGS IMPLEMENT A "PROBATIONARY ROLLOUT".
SABRETT
WE'RE ON A ROLL!
SABRETT
BUT, ODDLY...
FRESH HOT PRETZEL
ALL BEEF HOT DOG
...PEOPLE SEE THE MARK IN MORE INSTANCES THAN IT IS ACTUALLY PLACED.

OH, THE YOUTUBE VIDEO OF THE CLOUD OVER MANHATTAN IS QUICKLY OUTED AS THE FRUIT OF PHOTO-SHOP AND AFTER-EFFECTS.
THOUGH NOT BEFORE A HILARIOUS MASHUP WITH THE DOUBLE-RAINBOW GUY.

OH, GOD, LOOK AT THIS!! *SOB!*
AND SIXTY MILLION HITS.

STILL, THE MARK STARTS TURNING UP EVERYWHERE...IN OILY PUDDLES...
Instagram
peterwolfe2

twitpic
Ananda X. Pleizic
@anandaxpleizich
...LATTE FOAM...

...THE WRINKLES IN A FREEZE-FRAME OF THE TRAILER TO A LIAM NEESON THRILLER...
...BUT THE STRANGEST THING IS THE EFFECT IT HAS, PARTICULARLY, ON NEW YORKERS.
LIKE A SUMMER RAIN THAT CLEARS THE AIR...

IT INSPIRES NEW YORKERS TO *CHANGE.*
THAT'S RIGHT.
OKAY...

AS IF A NEW DAY HAS COME.
UH *HUH.*
YES.

WHOA, I DIDN'T KNOW YOU HAD A *GLOCK.*

IT'S ENOUGH TO MAKE ONE BELIEVE THERE IS *MAGIC* IN THE WORLD...
...MAGIC THAT CAN MOVE OUR *DESTINIES...*
JVC
IS PROUD OF
NEW
YORK
OUR CITY
...JUST A LITTLE.

OR MAYBE, FOR A FEW LITTLE PEOPLE...
...A LOT.
CHANEL
dancing with the Stars
Out of this World
BASKETBALL
JVC IS PROUD OF NEW YORK OUR CITY
Coca Cola
GET A PICTURE WITH IT BEHIND ME!
NO TURN
IT'S JUST SO -- NEW YORK!
WANT TO GET BOTH OF YOU IN A SHOT?
I CAN TAKE IT...

HAVE YOUR LAWYER LOOK IT OVER. IT SPELLS OUT THE PROFIT SHARING PLAN, ON TOP OF SALARY AND MEDICAL, MARY.
THIS IS YOUR OFFICE.
I-- DON'T KNOW WHAT TO SAY.

NO PORTFOLIO, NO SCHOOLING, NO AWARDS...
...AND SHE'S FREAKIN' GORGEOUS!
The New York Times Magazine
The Shy Beauty Who Gave the City Back Its Pride
by George Gustines
Mary Capolavoro

I'VE HEARD IT DISMISSED AS A "MELTING 'N'"--BUT I FIND THAT FLUIDITY CENTRAL TO ITS CHARM.
NONSENSE. IT'S THE STATUE OF LIBERTY AND MANHATTAN ISLAND --ELEGANTLY SIMPLIFIED.
I FIND IT SUGGESTIVE OF AN OSCILLOSCOPE. A SPIKE OF EXCITE-MENT, FOLLOWED BY A SURGE OF RELAXING BLISS--THAT'S NEW YORK!
NOT TO MENTION...
...A MODELLING OF MALE--THE PHALLIC SPIKE--AND FEMALE, A BREAST-LIKE CURVE. THAT'S NEW YORK, TOO!

I'M SO SORRY, JOSH, I CAN'T... THEY WANT ME HERE FOR INTERVIEWS.
THEY'RE HIRING DESIGN STAFF BECAUSE OF ALL THE NEW ACCOUNTS.
WELL, BECAUSE OF *ME,* THEY SAY.
WOULD SUNDAY WORK?

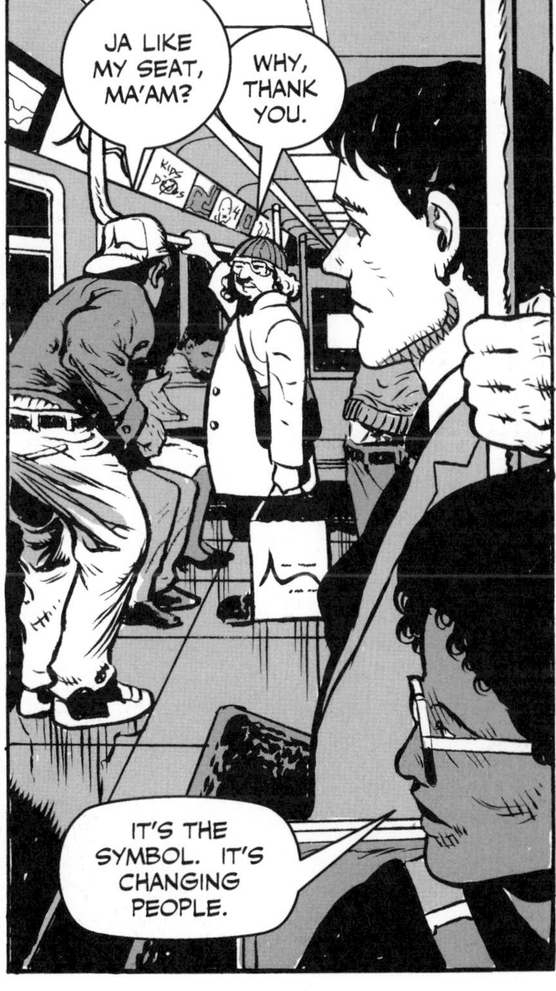

JA LIKE MY SEAT, MA'AM?
WHY, THANK YOU.
IT'S THE SYMBOL. IT'S CHANGING PEOPLE.

IT'S THE MARK THAT INSPIRED ME, SO I WEAR IT TO INSPIRE OTHERS.
I'M GONNA RUN THE NEW YORK MARATHON THIS FALL, IS MY GOAL.
I'VE HEARD APPLICATIONS ARE WAY UP.
ISRAEL CRISIS
FOODS THAT BOOST SEX
THE UN-MOVIES
TIME
Can a Logo Change the Human Heart?
IT'S BEAUTIFUL WORK. LET ME TALK WITH, AH, WITH MY COLLEAGUES.
THERE'S MORE AT MY WEBSITE.
I COULDN'T FIND YOURS.
BRRRING!
YES, I'VE GOT TO GET THAT DONE.
IT'S BEEN SUCH A WHIRLWIND!

EXCUSE ME. YES?
MARY? CAN YOU COME TO MY OFFICE AND PROOF-READ YOUR CARDS?
CERTAINLY, MS. NOLAN.

THEY'RE... PERFECT.
"SENIOR CREATIVE DIRECTOR"?
YOU WERE EXPECTING "VICE PRESIDENT," PERHAPS?
GLURKLE GLURP
nolan&briggs

JUST THE OPPOSITE!
I MEAN TO DO MY BEST, MS. NOLAN, BUT I'M NERVOUS.
I DIDN'T GO TO SCHOOL FOR THIS.
MY COMPUTER SKILLS, FOR ONE...
OH...

PLENTY OF PEOPLE CAN HELP WITH THAT.
IF YOU HIT IT OFF WITH ONE OF THE INTERVIEWEES, CHOOSE THEM TO EXECUTE YOUR IDEAS.
THAT'S TACTICALLY WISE--ENVY FOR YOUR SUDDEN RISE EXISTS HERE.
SO PICK SOMEONE GRATEFUL TO YOU.

I FEEL LIKE I'VE WON THE LOTTERY WITH A TICKET I FOUND ON THE SIDEWALK.
THE WORK YOUR PRESENCE DRAWS TO US AMPLY JUSTIFIES YOUR SALARY.
BELIEVE ME, YOU'RE WORTH IT.
GLURKLE GLURP
WE NEED YOUR TASTE, AND YOUR PRESENCE IN BOTH CLIENT MEETINGS AND PRESENTA-TIONS.
THE HANDS-ON GRAPHIC DESIGN GRUNT WORK IS EASILY SEEN TO.

Photoshop File Edit Image Layer Select
Angelo F. Musso
Bail Bonds
SURE, I CAN MAKE THE NAME BIGGER.
BETTER. YEAH, THAT'LL DO.
LOOK, KID.
I'M GONNA HAVE TO PAY YOU IN MONTHLY CHUNKS.
IT'S SLOW.
KNOW WHAT HAPPENED LAST NIGHT AT THE MIDTOWN STATION?
COUPLE'A GANG BANGERS PLOP A GROCERY BAG ON THE DESK.
FULL'A GUNS!

THEY'RE GIVIN' 'EM UP BECAUSE "THEY MIGHT INJURE ANOTHER HUMAN BEING."
CRIME'S DOWN CITY-WIDE.
THAT'S GREAT, BUT BAD FOR ME.

YOU KNOW WHAT IT IS, RIGHT?
DON'T SAY IT!
IT'S THE MARK!
HEY, COULD WE USE IT IN MY LOGO?
NO. IT'S A REGISTERED TRADEMARK.
SOMETHING CLOSE, THEN.

SORRY, DADDY! LONG CREATIVE MEETING THIS MORNING.
MY LITTLE GIRL, THE EXECUTIVE!
SO GOOD OF YOU TO FIT US IN.
NOT SO LONG AGO YOU WORRIED YOU'D HAVE TO SUPPORT HER UNTIL SHE MARRIED.

LUNCH...
...IS ON ME.
DON'T GIVE YOUR FATHER A STROKE.
NO, I LIKE BOMBSHELLS! GIVE ME ANOTHER!

HOW'S JOSH TAKING THIS SUDDEN CELEBRITY?
JOSH IS UPSTATE AT A SKILLS CLINIC.
HE GETS BACK TODAY, THOUGH.

AND?
AND I THINK I'LL HAVE THE FRENCH ONION SOUP.
LOOK, IF DEVELOPMENTS HAPPEN, I'LL LET YOU KNOW.

IF THAT MAN WERE TO TREAT YOU LIKE ONE OF HIS SPORTS GROUPIES, I'D...
THAT IS SO NOT JOSH! HIS TEAM-MATES KID HIM ABOUT HOW SELF-RESTRAINED HE IS ON THE ROAD.

THEY CALL HIM "THE MONK."
THERE AREN'T --PROBLEMS IN YOUR RELATIONSHIP, ARE THERE?

I'VE READ THAT DUE TO INJURIES, A MUCH HIGHER PERCENTAGE OF PROFESSIONAL ATHLETES...
WE DO *NOT* HAVE PROBLEMS, MOTHER.

NOT THAT WAY, AT LEAST.
LOOK, CAN WE CHANGE THE TOPIC?
DADDY'S FOREHEAD VEIN IS BULGING.

HOW'S MAGDA?
MAGDA'S FINE, THOUGH HER TASTE IN MEN IS AS BAD AS EVER.
WEIRD OLD LEON LEFT HER FOR A STRIPPER.
NOT THAT SHE'S CRUSHED, BUT IT'S SO INSULTING!
ANYWAY, SHE GOT A RAISE, SO MAYBE SHE CAN PAY THE BACK RENT SHE OWES ME.
THAT IS, *YOU.*

THANKS FOR THAT.
IT'S THE ONE PART OF THIS THAT I CAN FEEL PURELY GOOD ABOUT...THAT I CAN MOVE BEYOND DEPENDING ON YOU FOR...
...FOR EVERYTHING.

WHAT PARTS AREN'T SO PURE?
WELL, THE FACT THAT I KNOW NOTHING ABOUT GRAPHIC DESIGN, FOR ONE.
THAT'S A PROBLEM I NEED TO SOLVE.

HOLD THE ELEVATOR!

THANKS.
JETS
I'M GOING TO TWENTY, TOO.
22?

NO, *ALSO* TWENTY.
DO I KNOW YOU?

NO, THOUGH I SUSPECT WE'RE GOING TO SEE THE SAME PERSON.
WAIT, YOU KNOW MARY?

NO, I'M INTERVIEWING FOR A JOB.
WITH HER.
BUT I READ SHE'S DATING YOU IN THE TIMES THING.
OHHH...
WELL, GOOD.
GOOD LUCK.

nolan & brig
JETS
OH, MR. TIEFENWASSER! I'LL TELL HER YOU'RE HERE.

MENTION THAT HER 3:00 APPOINTMENT, CAL RUPP, IS HERE, TOO.
OH.
I WILL.
JOSH!
PLURKLE PLISH
WELL.
ALPHA DOG MARKS HIS TERRITORY.
YOU'D BETTER KEEP HIM AWAY FROM THE FURNITURE.

PLURKLE PLISH
GOOD THING THEY DIDN'T HEAR YOU.
I THINK.
HAVE A SEAT.

MAYBE I'LL BENEFIT FROM POST-COITAL GLOW.
MR. RUPP? YOU CAN GO IN, NOW.

TEN MINUTES?
FIFTEEN.
I PROMISE.
I'LL GET YOU.

polan
SHE'LL SEE YOU NOW.

MAKE IT "TO MONA."
"TO MONA, WHO THRILLED ME."
HA HA!

SO NICE TO MEET YOU.
YOU MADE QUITE AN IMPRESSION ON JOSH.
ME, TOO!

I DID?
HE PRACTICALLY TOLD ME TO HIRE YOU.

HUH.
YUP.
WELL.
LET'S SEE WHAT YOU BROUGHT.

SORRY!
THAT'S OKAY.

CAL EXPLAINS THE PROBLEMS BEING ADDRESSED BY HIS DESIGNS...
...AND HIS THINKING BEHIND THE SOLUTIONS.
FOR A LAYPERSON LIKE MARY, IT'S AN EDUCATION.
GRAPHIC DESIGN ISN'T ONLY TASTE AND DECORATION...
...IT'S A WAY TO COMMUNICATE BY ALLUSION, DRAWING FROM A THOUSAND STREAMS OF CULTURE.
YOU KNOW PHOTOSHOP?
PHOTOSHOP, ILLUSTRATOR, INDESIGN, AND I'M LEARNING AFTER EFFECTS.
THEY WANT THE SYMBOL INTEGRATED INTO THIS CROWD SCENE.
ANY IDEAS?
LET'S PUT IT ON A NEW LAYER, AND SELECT IT.
WE DESELECT SOME BYTES OUT OF IT...
...ADD BITS...
YOU SEE I'M SELECTING PEOPLE'S HAIR.

YOU'RE GOING TO REPLACE COLOR?
DOES SHE KNOW SHE'S BREATHING IN MY EAR?
LET'S DO VARIATIONS, INSTEAD.
LIGHTEN, LIGHTEN, MORE RED, MORE YELLOW...
HIDE SELECTION BORDER.

THEY'RE BLOND!
LIKE YOU HAD THEM STANDING IN THE PATTERN OF THE SYMBOL!
DIFFERENT SHADES OF BLOND.
ZOOM IN, DO A BIT OF CLEANUP, AND YOU'RE DONE.

YOU'RE HIRED, IF YOU CAN ACCEPT THE PAY PACKAGE THEY OFFER...
...OR 25% MORE, BUT DON'T TELL THEM I TOLD YOU.
YOU'LL BE WORKING WITH ME.
GREAT!

IT'S JUST AMAZING WATCHING CAL MANIPULATE IT SO QUICKLY. HE KNOWS JUST WHAT TO DO!
GOOD AT MANIPULATION, IS HE?

JOSH, REALLY. YOU'RE THE ONE WHO TOLD ME TO GIVE HIM A LOOK.
HE'S PROBABL GAY, ANYWAY.

WHAT MAKES YOU SAY THAT?
I DIDN'T GET THAT VIBE IN THE ELEVATOR.
JUST THAT A LOT OF PEOPLE IN THE ARTS ARE.
IT'S A WELCOMING FIELD FOR THEM.
AND FORGIVE ME IF I DOUBT THAT A PR FOOTBALL PLAYER HA WELL-TUNE GAYDAR.

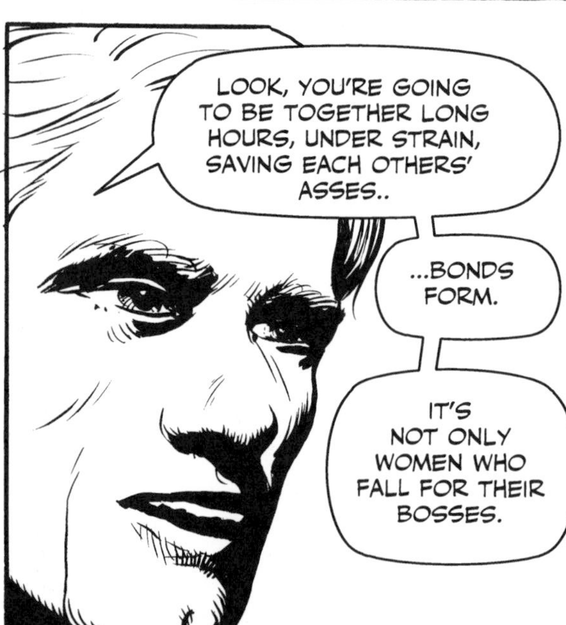
LOOK, YOU'RE GOING TO BE TOGETHER LONG HOURS, UNDER STRAIN, SAVING EACH OTHERS' ASSES..
...BONDS FORM.
IT'S NOT ONLY WOMEN WHO FALL FOR THEIR BOSSES.

WELL, IT'S NOT ME YOU NEED TO FEAR STRAYING.

WHAT DO YOU--
JOSH TIEFENWASSER!
IT'S SO WILD! WE WERE JUST TALKING ABOUT YOU!

SORRY, SWEETCAKES, BUT I'M WITH THE WOMAN I LOVE.
OH, SHE'S BEAUTIFUL... NATURALLY!
LOOK, HEY, I GET IT.

BUT IF YOU TWO WANT COMPANY, I'M GAME. HERE'S MY NUMBER.
THINK ABOUT IT.

PEOPLE LIKE YOU...
...GET TO BREAK RULES.
THE LOOK IN JOSH'S EYES, TO MARY, IS UNREADABLE...

GET YOUR HANDS OFF MY MAN, BITCH.

I GOTTA SAY...

I LIKE IT WHEN YOUR CLAWS COME OUT.

YEOW!

SORRY! SORRY!
IT'S OKAY.
JUST SURPRISED ME.
YOU'RE FULL OF SURPRISES.

NO, I'M NOT.
HEY, DON'T LEAVE.
NO. EXPLAIN.
I'M BORING, I KNOW.
TO SOMEONE LIKE YOU.

JOSH, IS IT SOMETHING YOU WANT?
ANOTHER PERSON HERE WITH US?
WHAT, DID THAT CAL GUY PITCH IT TO YOU?

NO, GOOFBALL.
THAT DITSY BIMBO!
OH, YEAH, HA.
SO I'M "DITZY!"

I KNOW IT'S THE BIG MALE FANTASY...
...AND GIVEN TONIGHT, AT THE RESTAURANT, STORIES ABOUT ATHLETES ARE TRUE.

WELL, A COUPLE THINGS, MAR.
FIRST, THE GIRLS THAT GUN FOR ME ARE USUALLY SKANKY, WHICH ISN'T MY TYPE...
...OR SUCH PREDATORY GOLDDIGGERS THAT THEY MIGHT AS WELL CARRY SHOVELS.

THE FACT YOU DIDN'T KNOW WHO I WAS WHEN WE MET?
I LOVED THAT.
AS FOR THE OTHER...

I'VE SEEN PLENTY OF GIRLS KISSING, AND IT'S GREAT.
BUT IF YOU FORCED YOURSELF INTO SOMETHING YOU WEREN'T ENJOYING...
...FOR ME...
...I'D HATE THAT.
NOW, I GOTTA TAKE A LEAK.

SQUEEEK

THE DOOR IS LOUDER THAN HE'D LIKE.

BUT MAGDA'S MEDITATION SEEMS UNDISTURBED.

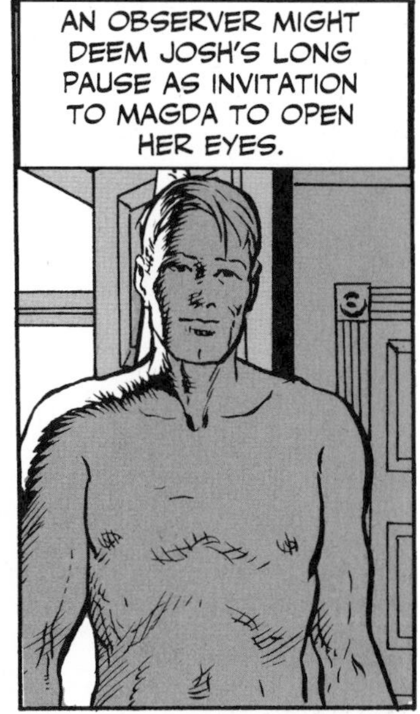
AN OBSERVER MIGHT DEEM JOSH'S LONG PAUSE AS INVITATION TO MAGDA TO OPEN HER EYES.

BUT HER BLISS ESCAPES THE JOLT OF MALE NAKEDNESS.

HER FACE, BATHED IN SHIFTING BLUE LIGHT, STAYS SERENE.

JOSH DOESN'T EVEN CONSIDER THE QUESTION THAT IT POSES...

WHO MEDITATES WITH A MUTED TV ON?

ALL RIGHT.
ON THE THIRTIETH, WE PRESENT CONCEPTS FOR PHASE II.
IF THEY LIKE IT, WE HAVE A GREAT THREE YEARS.
MAYBE FOUR.
IF THEY DON'T, IT'S OPEN TO COMPETITIVE BIDDING.
WE STILL MIGHT GET IT, BUT AT A LOWER LEVEL.
SO THIS IS IMPORTANT.
AS AN ASIDE, I WAS ON THE PHONE WITH SPIELBERG'S PEOPLE.

THEY WANT TO OPTION THE MARK TO BE THE BASIS FOR A MOTION PICTURE.

HOW'S *THAT* WORK?
BE A CG CHARACTER.
LOUIS CK CAN VOICE IT.

SO THIS THING'S GOT MOMENTUM.
DON'T LISTEN TO THE TALK THAT IT'S PEAKED TOO SOON.
THAT'S JUST RIVAL AGENCIES...

...SHOOTING ARROWS AT A JUMBO JET OVERHEAD.
WHOOPS!
BUT WE NEED A FAT, SEXY PRESENTATION WITH THE MARK IN EVERY CONCEIVABLE USAGE...
WHOA!
...TO SHOW WE SHOULD BE PILOTING THE PLANE.
KERASH!
HERE ARE YOUR WORK GROUPS AND ASSIGNMENTS.
THERE'S TASK OVERLAP.
YOU'RE IN COMPETITION.
EASY...
SON OF A SORE-KNEED STINKIN' BITCH!

HOPE THAT'S NOT AN OMEN.
NO, THAT'S ROLF.
IS HE OKAY?
GETCHER HANDS OFFA ME, YOU SPIDER-FINGERED GHOUL!
I THINK SO.

MOVING ON...
I'M THINKING AN EARTHWORK...
...LIKE ROBERT SMITHSON'S FAMOUS "SPIRAL JETTY."
IT'D PROJECT INTO THE EAST RIVER OFF BATTERY PARK.

OR HOW ABOUT A TOPIARY IN CENTRAL PARK?
NEAR THE FOUNTAIN!
OOOH...

YOU KNOW, LOOKING AT THIS LIST...
I DON'T SEE THE, WELL, LITTLE STUFF.

YOU KNOW... LIKE CITY STATIONERY, ENVELOPES...
...SUBWAY CARDS...
...CITY VEHICLES, LIKE METRO BUSES, SANITATION TRUCKS..
AM I BEING NAIVE?
YOU...
Coke

...ARE DOING WHAT THE REST OF THIS FIRM OF LILY-SNIFFING AESTHETES SHOULD'VE REMEMBERED *DAYS AGO.*
MY CITY CONTACTS WARNED ME THAT ONE OFFENDED DEPARTMENT COULD SCOTCH THIS DEAL.
YES, STATIONERY, TRUCKS, ALL OF IT, FROM CITY FINANCE TO DOGCATCHER TO DEPARTMENT OF ECOLOGY!

SHE'S NOT ONLY GOT A VISUAL MAGIC, SHE'S GOT OUR BACKS, TOO!
ACTUALLY, I --
ENOUGH!
THIS MEETING'S *OVER!*
LOOK, NOBODY GETS A HARDER STIFFY THAN ME AT BLUE-SKY BRAINSTORMING SESSIONS, BUT WE HAVE *WORK TO DO.*
WE NEED STATIONERY FROM EVERY CITY AGENCY. *IN HAND...*
WE MAY HAVE TO OVERPRINT EXISTING LETTERHEADS, SO WE NEED SAMPLES!
Coke

LOOK, CAL, I KNOW YOU ASKED ABOUT STATIONERY THIS MORNING...
HE CUT ME OFF.
HEY, IT'S OKAY. THE MOMENT PASSED.
I CAN TALK TO HIM...
I DON'T NEED A PAT ON THE HEAD!
ALL RIGHT.
CAN YOU CALL YOUR FRIEND IN CITY HALL FOR STATIONERY?
YES.
WHAT IS IT ABOUT SOME PEOPLE?
THE WORLD WANTS TO LOVE THEM.
AND IT MAKES UP REASONS TO DO SO.
I JUST DON'T GET IT.
IT HAS LESS MEANING THAN THE NIKE SWOOP.
IT'S A RORSCHACH BLOT.
BUT PEOPLE LOVE IT.
REMINDS ME OF THAT STEVE MARTIN INTERVIEW...
...HE SAID WE SOMEHOW AGREE THAT SOMEONE IS FUNNY, "AT THIS CULTURAL MOMENT."
MAYBE THAT'S ALL IT IS.
AN AGREEMENT TO BE CHARMED TOGETHER.
AND HOW LONG DOES THAT LAST?
JETS

YOU THE JANITOR NOW?

JOSH. HOW NICE.

HERE. LET ME HELP.
NO, I GOT IT.
PLEASE.

JEEZE, IT'S STICKY.
HERE, WATER WILL CUT IT.
GUY MAKES FOUR MIL A YEAR AND HE'S CLEANING A TABLE WITH ME?

OH. SORRY.

NO, IT WAS ME.
WHAT ARE YOU TWO UP TO?

BABYDOLL! I HAVE THE AFTERNOON OFF!
LET'S GET OUT OF HERE!
SORRY. WE JUST GOT ORDERS FOR THE BIG PUSH.
CAL AND I HAVE A MILLION THINGS TO DO.

JOSH, IT'S WORK!
I GOT YOU, MAR.
YOU GET MORE TIME WITH MY GIRL THAN I DO, ART MAN!
ACTUALLY, I HAVE TO GET TO CITY HALL AND BEG STATIONERY FROM TWENTY DEPARTMENTS.
WHAT'RE YOU DOING?!
I GOT YOU, MAR.
SOUNDS TEDIOUS. YOU THINK MY PRESENCE MIGHT BOOST COOPERATION?
WHAT AN EGO.
ACTUALLY, IT PROBABLY WOULD.
GREAT! LET'S ALL THREE OF US GO!
JOSH, I CAN'T. I HAVE TOO MANY -OOF!-
DINNER, THEN?
LATE. EIGHT?
THINK WE CAN MAKE THAT, CALVIN?
JUST "CAL" -- AND SURE.
"WE?"

ew York
ity Hall

CELEBRITY IS AN ODD POWER.
IT QUICKENS THE PULSE OF THE NUMBEST BUREAUCRAT.
CAN I GET YOUR AUTOGRAPH?
WOW.
SURE--GET SOME DEPARTMENTAL STATIONERY--A FEW SHEETS.
AND AN ENVELOPE!
JETS

EVENTUALLY...
WHAT NEXT?
THAT'S ALL OF THEM. THANKS FOR YOUR HELP.
JETS

THERE'S TIME TO KILL BEFORE MARY'S READY.
I FEEL LIKE A BEER. YOU GAME?
I GUESS SO.

MARY'S QUITE A GIRL, HUH?
THAT SHE IS.
LIKE HER?
SURE. UH... HOW DO YOU MEAN?

SO YOU'RE ATTRACTED.
I...KNOW SHE'S YOUR GIRL, JOSH.
I KNOW YOU DO, BUT THE HEART WANTS WHAT IT WANTS, RIGHT?

QUOTING WOODY ALLEN! SHEESH!
LOOK, YOU HAVE NO THREAT FROM ME, JOSH.

I MEAN, C'MON.
I'M NOT THREATENED. I LIKE YOU.
UH, WHY?
CLINK
MARY SAYS YOU'RE GOOD AT YOUR JOB.

I RESPECT MASTERY, WHETHER IT'S BROKEN FIELD RUNNING...
...OR, WHAT DO YOU CALL IT, COMPUTER ART?
GRAPHIC DESIGN.
OH.
OKAY, I'M IGNORANT.
I LIVE IN A BUBBLE.
EVER SINCE A SCOUT RECRUITED ME AT SEVENTEEN.
THEY'VE BEEN GROOMING YOU SINCE THEN?!

IT'S HOW IT WORKS.
ME AND A THOUSAND GUYS WHO DIDN'T MAKE IT.

MAKES YOU THE CRÉME DE LA CRÉME, I GUESS.

MAKES ME LUCKY I DIDN'T GET A CAREER-ENDING INJURY...
...OR FAIL A DRUG TEST AT A CRUCIAL TIME...
...OR LOSE OUT FOR A DOZEN OTHER REASONS.
WOULD YOU HAVE?

AAAH.

EVERYBODY'S GOT THINGS.
INCONVENIENT THINGS.
HOW ABOUT YOU, CAL?

HUH?
ANY STRETCHERS ON THE RESUME?
OR OTHER SKELETONS?
WHAT THE F--!
OKAY, EASY. YOU HAVE THE CHOPS, WE'VE ESTABLISHED.

HI, JOSH. I'M ANNA.
AND THIS IS SUKI.
HI.
WHO'S YOUR CUTE FRIEND ?

LET'S SEE IF MARY'S FINISHED EARLY.

YOU SURE ABOUT THIS?
INDULGE ME--I FEEL BAD ABOUT BLOWIN' OFF THOSE LADIES.
ONE HAD HER EYE ON YOU.
OH, I WASN'T INTERESTED.
MUCH.
JETS
OHHH... GOOD, THEN.
I'M TAKING "THE MARK" TEAM TO "PER SE" FOR DINNER.
FIVE CELEBRITY SIGHTINGS GUARANTEED!
CAB'S WAITING, MAR.
ALMOST READY.
NO SHOP TALK, NOW.
OH, JUST A LITTLE...
IS SHE PRESSING HER LEG AGAINST ME ON PURPOSE?

HELLO?
SLOW DOWN, MAGDA. WHAT?

HE USED A KNIFE TO CUT THE STRAP!
ALL MY CREDIT CARDS, CASH...
...EVEN MY DAMN DIAPHRAGM!
YES, IF YOU CAN...
NYP

SOON...
YOU SURE? I'M NOT GOING TO BE GOOD COMPANY TONIGHT.
'COURSE I'M SURE! IT'S JUST WHAT YOU NEED!
BESIDES, WE WERE SHORT ONE.
THIS IS CAL, BY THE WAY.
MARY'S GRAPHIC DESIGN BUDDY.
JETS

SORRY TO KILL THIS BOTTLE SO SOON...
...I'M STILL KIND OF UPSET.
OF COURSE.
WAITER! ANOTHER OF THIS!
DON'T WORRY, MAGDA. THEY'RE GOOD ABOUT REPLACING CARDS QUICKLY, AND YOU'RE NOT LIABLE FOR THE CHARGES.

COMFORTING.

MAYBE MY DADDY WILL SWOOP IN AND FIX EVERYTHING.
OR MY MILLIONAIRE BOYFRIEND.
UH OH.

OR MAYBE I'LL SCRATCH A MARK AND HAVE A DREAM JOB DROP IN MY LAP LIKE, OH, LIKE A DIAMOND NECKLACE DROPPED FROM AN AIRPLANE.

COME ON. SHE DOESN'T DESERVE THIS.
THAT'S THE WORSHT OF IT!
YOUR WINE.

FILL 'ER UP. THE NIGHT IS YOUNG.
YOU'RE RIGHT, CAL. SHE'S A NICE PERSON, ON TOP OF IT ALL.
YOU CAN'T EVEN FLUCKING HATE HER!

TO MARY, FOR WHOM GOD AND THE ANGELS SWEEP THE SIDEWALK IN FRONT OF HER FEETS.
WHILE WE MERE MORTALS STEP IN THE DOG CRAP.
IT IS A LONG DINNER.

WHICH FLOOR?
TEN.

GOD, I'VE BEEN SUCH A SHITCH...
...A SHIHT, TONIGHT...
WATCH IT.

SORRY YOU HAD TO ENDURE ME, CAL.

UH OH... I'VE MADE YOU MAD, MARY.
I KISS THE WRONG GUY GOOD-NIGHT?

I'M NOT MAD.
LET'S GET YOU TO BED.
GOOD IDEA.

I'LL TAKE CARE OF HER.
THIS A HABIT WITH HER?
NO.
GOD, YOU'RE STRONG.

I CUT MAGDA A LOT OF SLACK.
I CAME TO NEW YORK A CLUELESS LITTLE LAMB.
SHE SHOWED ME HOW TO COPE WITH THE CITY.
BUT SHE'S FRAGILE, IN SOME WAYS.
NOW WAIT HERE.

I'LL GET THAT BOOK WE TALKED ABOUT.
THIS IS ALL KIND OF INTENSE... *INTIMATE.*

RIGHT...DAVID CARSON. HE'S A CELEBRATED DESIGNER, BUT I'M NOT QUITE ON BOARD.
WHY'S THAT?

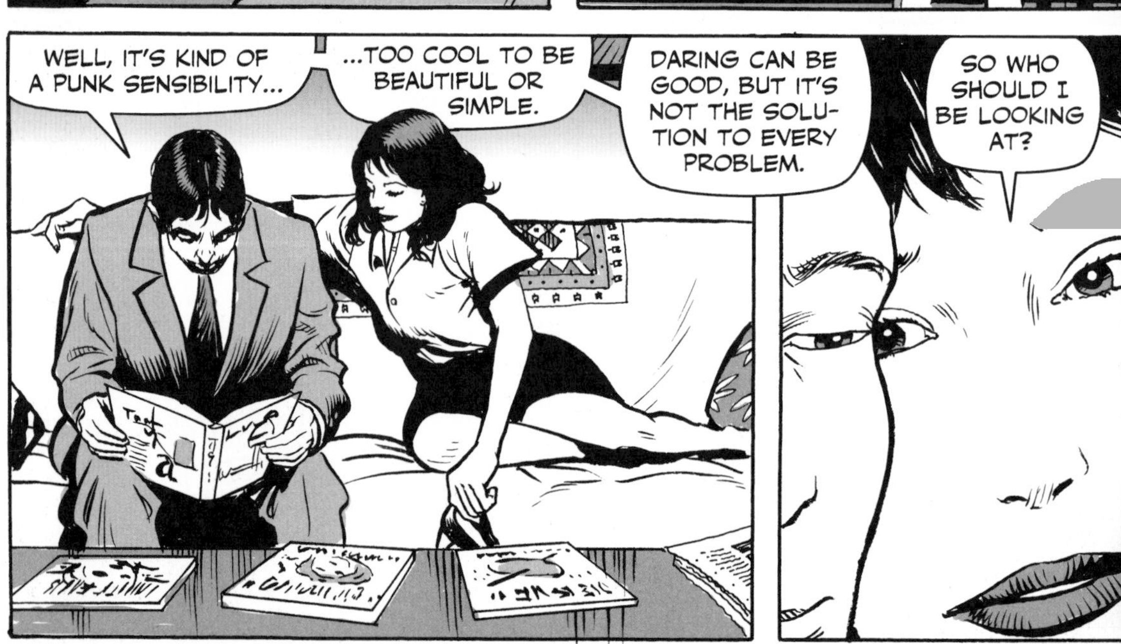
WELL, IT'S KIND OF A PUNK SENSIBILITY...
...TOO COOL TO BE BEAUTIFUL OR SIMPLE.
DARING CAN BE GOOD, BUT IT'S NOT THE SOLU-TION TO EVERY PROBLEM.
SO WHO SHOULD I BE LOOKING AT?

CHIP KIDD, MAYBE...
GOING BACK, MILTON GLASER, THE PUSH PIN GANG...
...MAYBE EVEN PAUL RAND.

LIKE YOU SAID, I SHOULD LEARN THE HISTORY OF THE FIELD.
I HAVE SOME BOOKS. I'LL BRING THEM IN.

CAL PAGES THROUGH THE BOOK.

A CERTAIN TENSION GROWS.

I'D OFFER YOU WINE BUT I THINK ALL OF US ARE A BIT, YOU KNOW...
OR WOULD YOU LIKE SOME?

JOSH, ARE YOU HAVING TROUBLE IN THERE?

I TOOK HER SHOES OFF BUT I STOPPED THERE.
DON'T WANT ANY MISTUNDER-- UNDERSTAND--
....DINGS.

C'MERE.
WHOO!

POOR KID.
I'M OKAY.
I MEANT HER. HAVING TO SQUINT AT YOUR DAZZLING HALO ALL DAY.

EVERYBODY HAS TO LEARN TO HANDLE ENVY.

WHAT DO YOU MEAN, CAL?
JUST WHAT I SAID.
CAL...

...YOU DON'T KNOW HOW GLAD I AM THAT YOU WALKED IN MY DOOR.

CAL DOES NOT REPLY.

SHE MEANS IT, PAL.
YOU TAKE GOOD CARE OF MY GIRL.
IT'S MY JOB.

YOU KNOW...

...I'M ON A TEAM WHERE WE HAVE TO MAKE EACH OTHER LOOK GOOD TO IN ORDER TO WORK.
I KNOW HOW IMPORTANT IT IS.
AND I APPRECIATE IT.

WELL, THANKS.
JOSH'S GRIP ON HIS ARM FEELS ODD...
...MARY'S, ELECTRIC.

THANK YOU.
A LONG MOMENT PASSES.
IT FEELS LIKE SHE'S GOING TO KISS HIM.

BUT IT'S TOO WEIRD A MOMENT TO BEAR.
JESUS, THAT MUST HAVE BEEN GOOD WINE.
THEY LAUGH.

I GOTTA GO.

SURE? DON'T WANT TO HANG OUT A WHILE?
NO, A LOT TO DO TOMORROW.
THANKS FOR THE GREAT DINNER.
YOU TWO SLEEP TIGHT.

YOU DON'T HAVE TO STOP...
...I'M CLOSE...
YOU KNOW...?
...I LIKE THAT DUDE.
YEAH...

ME TOO.
SOMEHOW, IT *ACTIVATES* SOMETHING IN THEM BOTH.

MILTON GLASER GRAPHIC DESIGN
MILTON GLASER
type
CHIP KIDD
WORK 1996-2006
BOOK ONE
paul rand
CLICK
MARY.

GOOD MORNING, MS. CAPOLAVORO.
nolan & briggs
MORNING, RACHEL.

HI, CAL.
CLIK.
CLIK.

I HOPE LAST NIGHT--
NO, IT WAS FUN.
CLIK.

SIGH
CLIK.

YOU TWO DO THAT STATIONERY YET?
JUST FINISHED.
WANT TO REVIEW THEM?
NAW. WITH MARY'S MARK, THEY'LL BE GREAT.
GOOD JOB, SWEETHEART.

I HATE IT WHEN HE CALLS ME SWEETHEART.
CAL.
WHAT?

THE DAYS TICK BY...
THE PRESENTATION FILLS OUT.
THE BEHAVIOR OF NEW YORKERS CONTINUES SOMEWHAT ASKEW...
WHY AM I DOING THIS?
MY GOD, YOU'RE JOSH TIEFEN-WASSER!
GYROS · FALAFEL
TIPS
CITY BUSINESS IS SIMILARLY AFFECTED.
A5
New, Old-Style Streetlights May Be Obsolete
ADDING "MARK" PROPOSED
By GEORGE GUSTINES
Thousands of new, historically evocative streetlights purchased by the city may be retrofitted with the popular abstract mark that seems on track to officially be adopted as a new symbol of the city.
The lamps, a pet project of the Mayor, are based on an original turn-of-the-century design by Mortimer
MARY, LOOK. YOU'RE CONQUERING THE WORLD.
MS. NOLAN, HOW DO I BUDGET THE FREELANCER PART OF THE PROPOSAL PRESENTATION?
"BUDGET." WHAT A QUAINT CONCEPT.
WELL, LET ME SHOW YOU OUR SYSTEM.

CAL RUPP.
OH, HI, JOSH.
YEAH, CAL. WONDERED IF YOU'D LIKE TO CATCH THIS EXHIBITION GAME THIS WEEKEND--AS MY GUEST, IN THE TEAM SKYBOX.
I...THOUGHT MARY WAS GOING UP FOR HER MOM'S OPERATION THIS WEEKEND.
YEAH, SHE IS. BUT YOU'RE WELCOME TO COME. THE AFTER-GAME DINNER'S A FANCY DEAL, AND INTERESTING.
WELL...THANKS. BUT I THINK I'LL HAVE TO TAKE A RAIN CHECK.
BUT THANKS.
THAT WAS JOSH.
DID YOU ASK HIM TO INVITE ME?
NO...
WHAT, YOU THINK I'M TRYING TO MANIPULATE YOU?
DESIGN
I'M NOT.
CHI

I THINK IT'S GENIUS. SHE DESERVES ALL THE FUSS.
I MEAN, IF YOU CAN SUM UP NEW YORK WITH A SYMBOL THAT **FEELS** GOOD, THAT'S A MINOR MIRACLE!
I DON'T KNOW. I THINK I'M KIND OF GETTING OVER IT.
DON'T EVEN SAY THAT!
IF YOU'VE GOT LIGHTNING IN A BOTTLE, DON'T OPEN THE CAP!
I MEAN, WHAT WOULD WE DO IF PEOPLE STOPPED LIKING IT?!
YEAH.
WHAT **WOULD** WE DO?

TAXI!
TAXI!!
DAMN!
WHAT DOES IT TAKE?
HEY, CAL! HOP IN!
GET OUT OF THE HEAT!
JOSH?!
I'M--I'M GOING TO BROOKLYN...
NO PROBLEM! I'VE GOT SOME TIME TO KILL.

AFTER AN AWKWARD CONVERSATION ABOUT SWEDISH DESIGN AESTHETICS...

I LIKE THE GHOST DUDE.
MUNCH. "THE SCREAM".
RIGHT.

SO YOU HAVE YOUR OWN BUSINESS, TOO, EH?
KIND OF ON HOLD AT THE MOMENT, BUT YEAH.
NOLAN AND BRIGGS IS A GREAT SHOP, BUT IT'S WEIRD BEING AN EMPLOYEE AGAIN.

WHAT, YOU LIVE HERE, TOO?!
HUMBLE!
HEY! DON'T GO BACK THERE!
MAN... I SOUND LIKE THE WIZARD OF OZ.

GUESS YOU PUT IT ALL INTO YOUR COMPUTER...
WELL, IT'S MY LIVELIHOOD.
AND THINGS HAVE BEEN TIGHT.

INVEST IN YOURSELF, I GET IT.
YOU GOING TO SET IT UP AND STUFF? WANT HELP?
IT'S INSTALLING SOFTWARE.
A ONE-MAN JOB.

RIGHT.
WELL, I SHOULD BE GOING ANYWAY.
THANKS AGAIN.
WEIRD!

JOSH!
HI, MAGDA.
MARY HERE?
SHE DIDN'T TELL YOU?
HER MOM ASKED HER TO STAY FOR ANOTHER DAY.
HER MOM OKAY?
OH, YEAH. MARY'S PRETTY SURE SHE'S JUST LONELY.
SHOULD'VE CHECKED ALL MY MESSAGES.
UM.
WELL, YOU WANT ME TO ASSEMBLE THIS STUFF?
COULD I HELP? I'M VERY MECHANICAL.
I'LL GET TOOLS.
YOU DON'T HAVE TO APOLOGIZE FOR THE OTHER NIGHT, BY THE WAY.
I KNOW IT WAS A ROUGH DAY.
YOU ARE SO SWEET!
I'M SORRY ANYWAY.
THIS IS GOING TO BE FUN!

TWO DAYS LATER
NO, JOSH, I'LL BE HERE LATE, BUT THAT'S SWEET OF YOU.
YES, HE IS.
UNTIL MIDNIGHT, AT THIS RATE.
WHAT WOULD YOU DO? DISTRACT US FROM FINISHING, MOST LIKELY.
MAYBE HE'D LIKE TO PUT A WEBCAM ON US.

HOURS PASS.
THE MOOD CHANGES, AND CHANGES AGAIN.

FATIGUE AMPLIFIES FEELING.
THAT'S NICE.
THAT'S *REALLY* NICE.

A TENSION GROWS.

SMALL VICTORIES THRILL.
THANKS.

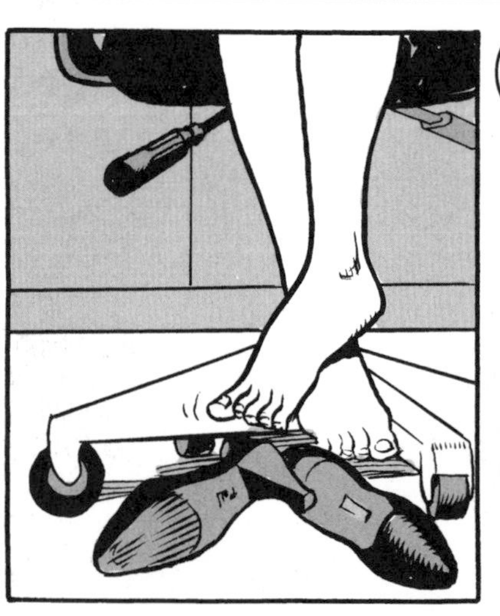

OH, MAN...

YET SOMETIMES TENSION, WHICH CANNOT BE ACTED ON AS THOSE WHO BEAR IT WOULD LIKE, PUSHES OUT WORDS...
IT'S BEAUTIFUL.
I LOVE... I LOVE IT.
AND THEY'LL LOVE YOU FOR IT.
...THAT BREAK THINGS.

CAL, WE'RE A TEAM.
CAL?

SORRY, I DIDN'T HEAR YOU.
THE JANGLING OF YOUR MOST-VALUABLE-PLAYER AWARDS IS SO LOUD.

I KNOW I GET TOO MUCH CREDIT.
I FEEL SICK EVERY TIME.

LIFE IS UNFAIR.

DAMN IT, ISN'T IT OUR JOB TO MAKE EACH OTHER LOOK GOOD?!
ISN'T IT?!

YOU WOULDN'T HAVE THIS JOB IF I HADN'T --
YES, BOSS.

I GUESS THAT'S THE BOTTOM LINE.
I GUESS IT IS.

GOODNIGHT.
GOOD NIGHT.

SHE HAS THE LOVE OF A FAMOUS MAN, OF HER EMPLOYER, OF THE WHOLE CITY.

PERHAPS IT'S THE HOUR, THE FATIGUE. WHY SHOULD CROSS WORDS WITH A HIRELING HURT SO MUCH?

YET SOMEHOW THEY DO.

WHY DID I DO THAT?
WHY DO I HAVE TO PISS IN THE PUNCH BOWL?

OH, CRAP, A BREAK-IN, HERE?!
I LEFT MY PHONE AT WORK, TOO!
CALVIN RUPP
DESIGN ASSOCIATES
GRAPHIC DESIGN
ADVERTISING

THE COMPUTER'S UNTOUCHED!
A MIRACLE!
BUT IT PROBABLY MEANS THEY'RE STILL HERE.
HE LISTENS.
HE HEARS A *GROWLING...*

NO, NOT GROWLING.
SNORING.
JOSH!

I FELL ASLEEP.
YOU DID ALL THIS?!
NOT ALL.
MOVERS HELPED.
A PLUMBER.

DAMN, I WANTED TO BE OUT OF HERE.
HOW'D YOU GET *IN?*
YOUR KEY.
OH YEAH.

SO WHY?
YOU KNOW, YOU DO SO MUCH FOR MARY, I THOUGHT I'D DO SOMETHING FOR YOU.
YEAH, LIKE ALL I DID FOR HER HALF AN HOUR AGO.

IKEA.
YEAH, I LIKE THAT SWEDISH DESIGN AESTHETIC.
LOOK, I KNOW THIS IS A BORDERLINE A-HOLE MOVE, BUT YOU HAVE TO ADMIT IT'S AN IMPROVEMENT.
31055

IT IS.
AND EVEN IF YOU HAD THE DOUGH, YOU WOULDN'T HAVE THE TIME.
TRUE.

SO IF YOU COULD LET THIS GO...
...JUST TAKE IT AS A FAVOR FROM A FRIEND, I'D BE RELIEVED.

OF COURSE. IT'S GREAT. THANK YOU.
THANKS.
I OWE YOU, THEN.
WHAT FOR? LOOKS LIKE I'M THE INDEBTED ONE.

WELL, IF YOU COULD FIND TIME TO COME ALONG SOME TIME...
...WITH ME AND MARY, I MEAN.
I'M NOT SURE SHE'D BE THRILLED WITH THAT

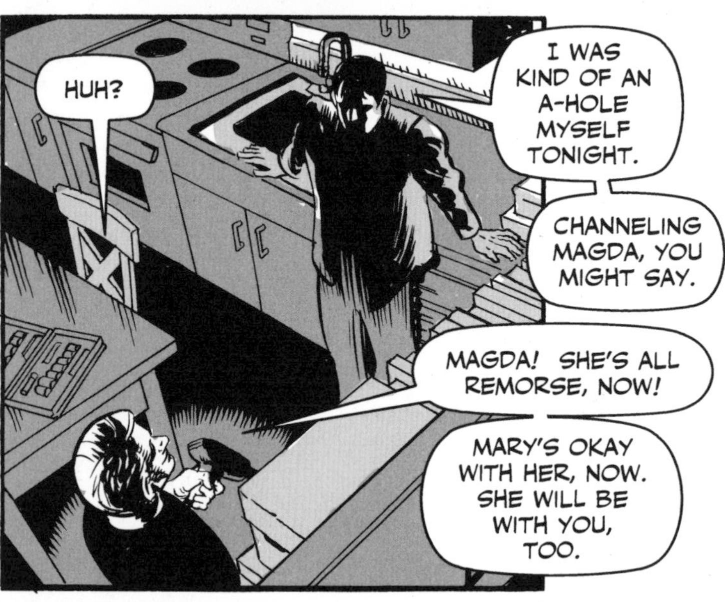
HUH?
I WAS KIND OF AN A-HOLE MYSELF TONIGHT.
CHANNELING MAGDA, YOU MIGHT SAY.
MAGDA! SHE'S ALL REMORSE, NOW!
MARY'S OKAY WITH HER, NOW. SHE WILL BE WITH YOU, TOO.

I CAN HANDLE MARY, YOU WATCH.
THINGS'LL BE KISSY-HUGGY WHEN I'M DONE.
G'NIGHT.

G'NIGHT.
CLIK!

WHY...
...DID I DO THAT?

WHAT IS *UP* HERE?
THE GUY HAS THE FAME, THE MONEY, THE GIRL TO DIE FOR.
COULD HE JUST BE ***LONELY?***
IS THAT EVEN ***POSSIBLE?***

MAN, HE SLEPT ON MY BED.
SO WEIRD, ALL OF THIS. I'M SO TIRED.

SLEEP, COME ON.
I WONDER IF HE GOT MARY THIS SAME BED.

SOME TIME LATER, IN WOODSTOCK, NEW YORK, WRINKLED HANDS CONTROL A FILE IN *FINAL CUT PRO.*
A FILE WHICH WILL INFLUENCE EVENTS.
AND DISSOLVE...
YES! A PERFECT FIT!
NOW, A PULL-BACK.
MARY, BABY, IT'S TOO BAD YOU'VE GOT TO GO DOWN...
...BUT YOU PICKED THE WRONG OLD HIPPIE TO SCREW OVER!
LATER YET, AT NOLAN & BRIGGS, MORE POWERFUL HANDS HOLD ANOTHER SORT OF INFLUENCE.
SWEET, HUH?
SO, HOW'S YOUR MOTHER DOING?
SHE'S RECOVERING JUST FINE. THANKS FOR ASKING.
NOW, HAS THE DIE-CUT BEEN ORDERED?

HEY, YOU TWO READY?
JOSH! IS IT 11:00 ALREADY?!
I ORDERED IT AT NINE.
POST-TIME'S AT ONE, SO WE'D BETTER MOVE IT.
MM.
LET ME USE THE LADIES' ROOM, AND WE'LL GO.

GLAD YOU'RE COMING, ART MAN.
WELL, THANKS FOR INCLUDING ME.

THEY SAID I COULD BRING UP TO FOUR FRIENDS, SO I DID.
WHO ARE THE OTHER TWO?
WELL...

HI, MAGDA.
OBOY.
HI, CAL.
HEY.
YOU GET THE PURSE THING WORKED OUT?

STILL WORKING ON IT, I'M AFRAID.
SOMEBODY IN KENYA HAD A GREAT TWO HOURS, THOUGH.
BUT THE BANK EATS THAT, RIGHT?

RIGHT. AND I'M DONE MOPING ABOUT THE REST, SO YOU CAN RELAX.
WELL, THAT'S A LOAD OFF MY MIND.
TOO ON THE NOSE?
JOSH, INTRODUCE CAL TO--

WALLACE RENFORT, TEAM PUBLICIST.
BUT I'M OTHERWISE A DECENT PERSON.
WHAT, THIS IS A JETS EVENT?

NO, I'M FREELANCING TODAY AT THE BEHEST OF JOSH'S AGENT.
THE MAN SOME-TIMES FAILS TO ARRIVE WHERE HE'S SUPPOSED TO BE IF THERE AREN'T GOAL-POSTS, OR 300-POUND LINEBACKERS TRYING TO KILL HIM.
SO I GET HIM, AND YOU FOLKS, FROM POINT A TO B TO C.
THIS IS OUR DRIVER, LEE

5 5
STAY IN LANE

SO ARE YOU A RACING FAN, JOSH?
I KNOW YOU CAN'T GAMBLE ON FOOTBALL, OF COURSE.
I NEVER GAMBLE.

I'M PRUDENT AS I CAN BE.
78% OF PRO FOOTBALL PLAYERS ARE BANKRUPT OR IN FINANCIAL STRESS WITHIN TWO YEARS OF RETIREMENT.
IT'S A BIT SKEWED, SINCE MOST PRO CAREERS LAST ONLY THREE YEARS. BUT STILL.
I'M MAKING HAY WHILE THE SUN SHINES AND SOCKING IT AWAY FOR MONSOON SEASON.
HENCE TODAY.

YEAH, WHAT *IS* THE DEAL TODAY?
PRETTY SWEET, REALLY.
A--STRICTLY CHASTE, I MUST STRESS--SORT OF ***HONEY TRAP.***
LURED BY THE CHANCE TO MINGLE WITH JOSH, RICH MEN WILL GATHER...
...TO BE WOOED TO JOIN IN A ***REAL ESTATE VENTURE.***

FOR EMPLOYING HIS MAGNETIC POWERS, AN INDECENT SUM WILL BE DEPOSITED INTO JOSH'S BANK ACCOUNT.
ALSO, HE'LL HAVE A TINY PERCENTAGE OF OWNERSHIP, SO THEY CAN BRAG THEY'RE "IN A DEAL WITH JOSH TIEFENWASSER."
THIS ISN'T A SCAM, IS IT?
I HOPE NOT.
I DON'T THINK SO.

KIND OF A RUDE THING TO SAY, CAL.
SORRY.
MY FAULT. I SPOKE FLIPPANTLY.
THIS IS JUST WHAT GULFSTREAM COMMUTERS DO TO MAKE BUSINESS FUN.

WHAT'S THE GUY'S NAME AGAIN, WALLACE?
LEETOLA. ROBERT LEETOLA.
BELMONT
NOW I'VE GOT DIRECTIONS TO HIS SKYBOX...SOMEWHERE HERE...

JOSH, OLD PAL!
BOB, SORRY I'M LATE.
"OLD PAL." I LOVE IT.
NO PROBLEM! AND THIS IS THE BEAUTIFUL MARY! AND...

INTRODUCTIONS ARE MADE, DRINKS POURED, THE PROCESS OF ESTABLISHING STATUS BEGUN.
SO, CAL, YOU'RE A TEAMMATE OF JOSH'S?
I DON'T RECOGNIZE YOU.
YEAH, I'M A ROOKIE. HAVEN'T GOTTEN OFF THE BENCH YET.

IF YOU DON'T MIND MY SAYING SO, YOU'RE SMALL FOR AN NFL'ER.
SMALL BUT FAST.
EH?

THEY CALL ME "ART MAN" BE-CAUSE MY RUNNING GAME IS A WORK OF ART.
HUH.

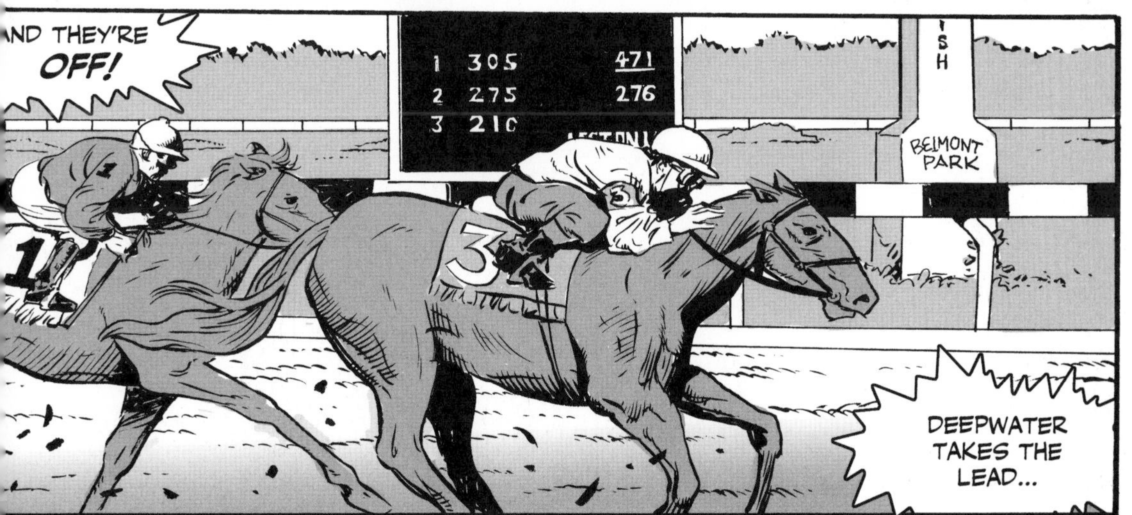
ND THEY'RE OFF!
1 305 471
2 275 276
3 210
BELMONT PARK
DEEPWATER TAKES THE LEAD...

PSST, MAR...
PSSPITSPSSIP SSITISSIPASS USSITISUSH WISSHISITIS

HA HA HA!
HEH.

AT THE HALF FURLONG IT'S DEEPWATER A LENGTH AHEAD OF LET 'ER RIP ON THE OUTSIDE...
CLOPPITA CLOPPITA CLOPPITA CLOPPITA CLOPPITA

I UNDERSTAND YOU HAVE A GULFSTREAM.
LEARJET 85, ACTUALLY.
I'M HEADING BACK TO MONTREAL ON IT TONIGHT.
MONTREAL! REALLY!

EVER BEEN THERE?
NEVER. THOUGH I KNOW WHAT POUTINE IS.
HAH! WELL, STAY AWAY FROM IT IF YOU WANT TO KEEP THAT PRETTY FIGURE.

AND IT'S LET 'ER RIP BY A NOSE!
INISH
MASTERPIECE SECOND, DEEPWATER THIRD, WITH KID STRONG FOURTH.
BELMONT PARK

WE'RE GOING DOWN TO PLACE BETS.
WANT TO COME?
NO, THANKS.

SO, CAL, YOU IN THIS THING?
THE DEAL? HECK, NO.
I'M JUST ALONG FOR THE FUN.

WELL, I'M MIGHTY IMPRESSED WITH WHAT YOUR FRIEND JOSH IS DOING.

TWO MILLION FIVE IS A REAL COMMITMENT.
HUH. REALLY.

UM, I HADN'T HEARD THAT.
I DIDN'T KNOW JOSH HAD *ANYTHING* IN THIS DEAL.
WHY'D HE *BE HERE,* OTHERWISE?

YEAH.

DUE DILIGENCE AND ALL THAT.

WHAT'RE YOU SAYING?

I'M NOT GOING TO SAY MORE THAN THAT, SMART GUY.
I DON'T KNOW.
HEY, LET'S EAT.

AS THE AFTER-NOON WEARS ON, CAL AVOIDS THE INVESTORS.
HE OBSERVES JOSH, WHO WEARS HIS CHARISMA AS EASILY AS AN OLD, FAVORITE SWEATER.
JOSH REFLECTS AND RESTATES THINGS PEOPLE SAY TO HIM.
HE LISTENS.
HE TELLS A TALE NOW AND THEN, BUT NEVER CASTING HIMSELF AS THE HERO.
AND, REALLY, HE REVEALS ALMOST NOTHING ABOUT HIMSELF.
AS IF BY HABIT.

AND IT'S LONG DIVISION!
THAT-- THAT'S MY HORSE!
AND MINE!

SIXTEEN-TO-ONE ODDS...THAT MAKES IT...
YOU JUST MADE $235!

YAY!
WAIT -- I THOUGHT I BET ON LONG DIVISION...
OH, CRAP.

WILL YOU HELP ME COLLECT MY WINNINGS?
SURE.
WHY? EVERY TIME!

CAL, LET ME LAY DOWN A BET FOR YOU.
SOMETHING WE CAN CHEER FOR TOGETHER.
NO...
COME ON, JUST TEN DOLLARS.

LOOK, THERE'S EVEN A HORSE NAMED CALVIN!
IT'S AN OMEN!
PROBABLY A BILL WATTERSON FAN.
SURE, FINE.

A HUNDRED ON CALVIN IN THE FIFTH.
A HUNDRED! THAT'S NOT WHAT YOU SAID!
HUSH. YOU KNOW I'M INSANELY LUCKY.

"LUCK BE A LADY TONIGHT."
LET'S GO IN THE STANDS -- I WANT CHEERING CROWDS AROUND US.

I'VE MADE A DECISION, CAL.
WHAT'S THAT?
I'M NOT GOING TO FEEL GUILTY ABOUT ALL THIS GOOD LUCK COMING MY WAY.
HAVE YOU?

TERRIBLY.
AND I'VE BEEN TRYING MY HARDEST TO STOKE THAT FIRE.
IT WOULDN'T WORK IF I DIDN'T ALREADY FEEL THAT WAY.
I'M SORRY ANYWAY.

I'VE BEEN SMALL.
YOU KNOW WHAT CHANGED?
WHAT?

MY MOTHER. HER CANCER.
IS IT WORSE THAN YOU'RE SAYING?
THEY THINK THEY GOT IT IN TIME, BUT YOU NEVER KNOW. IT JUST TELLS ME TO ENJOY THE GOOD LUCK, BECAUSE THE BAD COMES JUST AS EASILY.

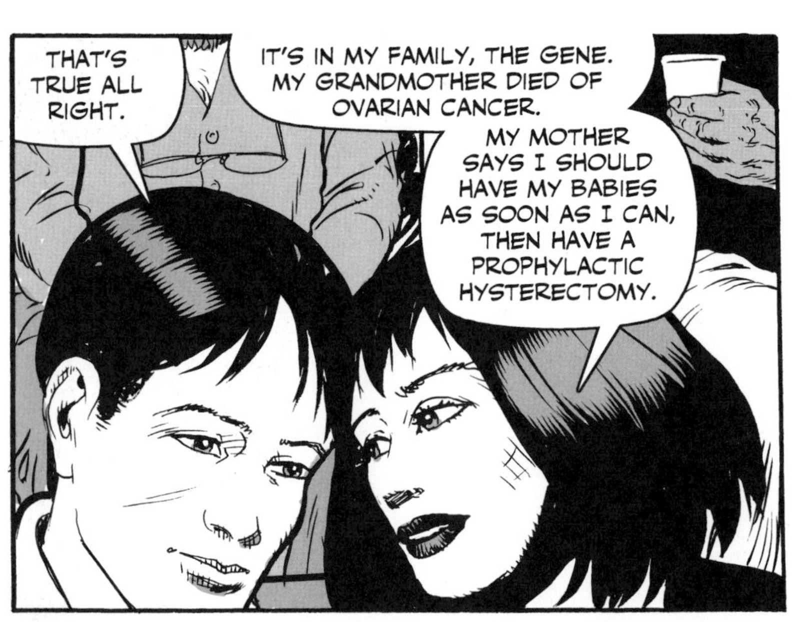
THAT'S TRUE ALL RIGHT.
IT'S IN MY FAMILY, THE GENE. MY GRANDMOTHER DIED OF OVARIAN CANCER.
MY MOTHER SAYS I SHOULD HAVE MY BABIES AS SOON AS I CAN, THEN HAVE A PROPHYLACTIC HYSTERECTOMY.

JOSH KNOW THIS?

JOSH AND I ARE NOWHERE NEAR HAVING THIS DISCUSSION.
IT'S ONLY THE LAST FEW WEEKS I'VE SEEMED IMPORTANT TO HIM.
AND HE SEEMS UNSETTLED... LIKE SOMETHING'S GOING ON IN HIM THAT HE DOESN'T UNDERSTAND.
ANYWAY, I'M NOT EVEN SURE I'LL TAKE MY MOTHER'S ADVICE. YOU HAVE TO TAKE CHANCES IN LIFE.
AND THEY'RE O

TAKING THE LEAD, IT'S *CALVIN!*
HEY!

LONG STORY IS MOVING OUT FOR RACING ROOM...
CALVIN FIRST, LONG STORY SECOND, KELLY'S PRIDE THIRD, WEBDING FOURTH --

IN THE SECOND FURLONG...
I CAN'T BELIEVE IT...
GO CALVIN!!

LOOK AT THEM GO!
LONG STORY GAINING...
IT'S CALVIN AND LONG STORY, NECK AND --

D IT'S LONG STORY BY A QUARTER LENGTH!
CALVIN SECOND, VEBDING THIRD...
WELL, DARN.
ALMOST.

WELL, THANKS ANYWAY--THAT REALLY DOES GET YOUR BLOOD GOING.
GUESS THAT'S WHY RACING IS SO POPULAR.
MY PURSE SPILLED.

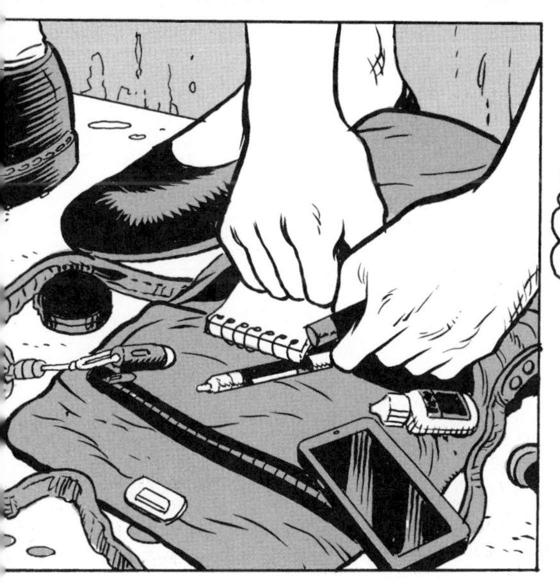

WOMEN DO HAVE TO DEAL WITH A LOT OF STUFF WE DON'T.
NO WONDER MAGDA WENT AROUND THE BEND AT DINNER.
SHOULD I OFFER HELP?
THOSE THINGS SEEM TOO INTIMATE TO TOUCH.

WE'D BETTER REJOIN THEM.
I GUESS.

HUH.
COULD THEY HAVE LEFT FOR DINNER?
IT'S EARLY FOR THAT...

CALL JOSH, WHY DON'T YOU?
DAMN -- MY PHONE'S DEAD. THE SPILL, MAYBE?
THEY'RE SUPPOSED TO BE TOUGHER THAN THAT.

I'LL CALL. WHAT'S HIS NUMBER?
I DON'T KNOW. IT WAS ON MY PHONE.
AND IT'S LISTED NOT UNDER HIS NAME, I KNOW, BUT AS HIS LLC CORPORATION WHICH IS SOME ACRONYM I CAN'T RECALL.
MAYBE WE SHOULD JUST MEET THEM AT THE RESTAURANT.

SURE, WHY NOT?
AN HOUR OR SO JUST THE TWO OF US.
LET'S GO SEE HOW TO GET TO THE TRAIN.
I GUESS WE COULD CALL MAGDA, BUT WHY BOTHER?

NOT TOO BUSY.
WE'RE GOING THE OPPOSITE WAY AS THE RUSH.

IF ONLY LIFE COULD ALWAYS BE LIKE THAT.
CONTINUING OUR THEME...
WHAT'S THAT?
LUCK. FICKLE LUCK.

HOW HAS LUCK SHAPED YOUR LIFE, CAL?
WELL, MY FAMILY WAS PRETTY NORMAL...EXCEPT FOR THE HEROIN AND THE NAZI THING.
I'M SERIOUS.

NO, MY FOLKS WERE GREAT. MY DAD HAD A BUSINESS FAIL, BUT HE GOT A JOB AND MOM BECAME A REALTOR, SO IT WORKED OUT.
I GUESS...
...I GUESS I SHOULD BE AS FORTHCOMING AS YOU WERE.

I WENT THROUGH A BAD TIME IN HIGH SCHOOL.
I HAD A BUDDY WHO DIED IN THE DUMBEST SPEEDBOAT ACCIDENT EVER.
HE HAD BINOCULARS AROUND HIS NECK, AND THEY GOT TANGLED IN THE WHEEL.
AND--?

HE SWERVED-- STILL NOT SURE WHY, MAYBE TO SCARE SOME WATER BIRDS.
ANYWAY, THE BINOCS STRAP TIGHTENED, HE DROVE INTO A ROCK, AND HE WAS THROWN.
THE STRAP BROKE HIS NECK. THE ONLY PERSON TO BE *HANGED* AT SEA SINCE BILLY BUDD.

HOW AWFUL.
IT SEEMED PRETTY DAMNED RANDOM AT THE TIME.
I STARTED DOING ANGRY, STUPID STUFF.
DRIVING LIKE A MANIAC, TAKING RISKS.
I HALF-BURNED DOWN A WOODWORKING SHOP. JUST CARE-LESS, MORONIC BEHAVIOR.
WOULD YOU CALL IT SURVIVOR GUILT?
MORE, LIKE, NOTHING MATTERED.
ANYWAY, I WAS HEADED FOR DEATH OR JAIL.
BUT SOMETHING HAPPENED. MY ART TEACHER HAD A BUDDY, A GRAPHIC DESIGNER.
A LIFELINE FOR ME.
HE LET ME HANG OUT IN HIS STUDIO, DO LITTLE JOBS, LEARN THE TOOLS, THE BUSINESS.
HE HELPED ME CREATE A PORTFOLIO THAT GOT ME INTO SVA ON SCHOLARSHIP.
I OWE THAT GUY.
MARY SPEAKS OF HER MENTORING FROM DOROTHY NOLAN.
MILES RACE BY.
THE PASSAGE TO MANHATTAN REACHES ITS FINAL LEG.
THE NOISE AND STROBING OF THE TUNNEL ENDS THE CONVERSATION.
BUT SOMEHOW, NOT ITS INTIMACY.

AT THE RESTAURANT.
I'M TERRIBLY SORRY, BUT MR. LEETOLA CALLED TO CANCEL THE DINNER.
PERHAPS HE COULDN'T REACH YOU?
SHOULD WE GET A TABLE?

WELL, I WONDER WHAT GIVES.
NOTHING GOOD, I IMAGINE. I HOPE JOSH IS OKAY...
JUST AS WELL THEY COULDN'T SEAT US.
I'VE READ ABOUT THIS PLACE. THE "CHEF'S TASTER MENU" STARTS AT $295 -- BEFORE DRINKS.

TIME WARNER CENTER
I KNOW A LITTLE PLACE NOT FAR FROM HERE...
LET'S!

SHOULD WE CALL? I KNOW MAGDA'S NUMBER.

I'M ENJOYING MYSELF THIS WAY. THEY DON'T NEED US.
I GUESS YOU'RE RIGHT.

NOBODY CALLED ***ME.***

THEY HEAD TO THE RESTAURANT IN NO HURRY.
THE EVENING IS GENTLY WARM.
THE RESTLESS ENERGY OF NEW YORK ON FRIDAY NIGHT HUMS WITH PROMISES.

MARY SAYS SOMETHING FUNNY.
IT'S *REALLY* FUNNY.
BECAUSE IT'S A JOKE ONLY CAL COULD GET, A REFERENCE TO A CONVERSATION A MONTH AGO.

CAL COUNTERS WITH ANOTHER INSIDE JOKE.
THEIR CONVERSATION CONTINUES IN THIS TACIT, ALLUSIVE WAY.
IT MAKES A HEADY CLOSENESS, WHAT IT MIGHT BE LIKE HAVING BEEN MARRIED LONG YEARS, SHARING REFERENCES AND MEMORIES THAT ALLOW A SHORTHAND NO OUTSIDER COULD FATHOM.
pollinaise

AND THEN...
LOOK, ONE OF THE NEW STREETLIGHTS GOT PUT UP EARLY.
HMM, IT NEEDS SOMETHING.
CAN'T PUT MY FINGER ON IT.

THEY DON'T EVEN LAUGH.
THE MOMENT IS TOO FRAGILE TO TOUCH, SUDDENLY.

THEY LOOK AT EACH OTHER, THE DEEP SHADOWS CARVING THEIR FACES INTO OBJECTS OF MYSTERY AND GLAMOUR.
CITY NOISE RECEDES, AS IF THE BENIGN HURRICANE OF NEW YORK LIFE HAS ITS STILL, QUIET EYE RIGHT HERE.
SOMETHING INVISIBLE GROWS *TAUT*...
...AND THEY SENSE WHAT HAPPENS NEXT WILL BE ENORMOUS, UNIVERSE-FILLING.

CAL, YOU SON OF A BITCH!!
ELRY

I--I DIDN'T TOUCH HER!
JOSH!
CONTRA TEMPS
BEST VALUE
YOU TOLD THAT GUY IT WAS ALL A SCAM!
WHY?

I DID NO SUCH THING!
WELL, HE SAID YOU TOLD HIM LEETOLA WAS LYING!
ALL I SAID WAS I DIDN'T KNOW YOU WERE IN FOR TWO AND A HALF MILLION OF YOUR OWN MONEY!
I'M NOT! WHAT DIFFERENCE DOES THAT MAKE?

APPARENTLY LEETOLA--
ALL I KNOW IS THESE GUYS SUDDENLY TURNED ON LEETOLA AND ME LIKE A BUNCH OF PIRANAS!
THEY WANTED S.E.C. FILINGS, CREDIT CHECKS, CORPORATE REGISTRATIONS, ALL SORTS OF...
...WELL, UNTIL THEY DIDN'T.
THEY ALL BAILED--IT'S OVER, GONE.

INCLUDING MY FEE, SINCE LEETOLA BLAMES ME FOR BRINGING YOU.
UNLESS I SUE HIM, ON A HANDSHAKE DEAL.
MAYBE YOU SHOULD.

IT IS NOT A MOMENT OF SOBER REFLECTION.
SO MUCH IS SWIRLING ABOUT.
MONEY.
REPUTATION.
MISMATCHED STATUS.
DENIED ATTRACTION.
THE WOMAN.

THANKS FOR THAT ADVICE.
YOU COMING, MAR?
NYC
TAXI

SAME AS EVER.
THEY GO WITH THE ALPHA DOG, EVERY TIME.

AFTER A DINNER OF STRAINED CONVERSATION AT WHICH THE DISASTER IS MINUTELY REHASHED...
WAIT HERE.

YOU'RE NOT STAYING?
YOU THINK I'D BE GOOD COMPANY TONIGHT?
NO, YOU SLEEP TIGHT.
I'LL CALL YOU WHEN THIS LAVA IN MY BRAIN COOLS.

MAGDA?

HUH.

THE END OF A PERFECT DAY.
POOR JOSH.

CAL.

IT'S ME. I'LL BE THERE IN TEN.

MONDAY, LUNCHTIME.
HA HA HA HA HA HA.

HA HA HA...
SO, OTHER USES...

HA HA HA HA HA HA
BUTT STITCHING ON BLUE JEANS.

A TASTEFUL ADDITION TO TRUMP TOWER.

NEW YORK CITY DOUCHE...
OFFICIAL NEW YORK CITY
douche
For Her
Not just on Wall Street any more.

AND LAST BUT NOT LEAST...
SHARK JUMP RAMP!
WHY LOOK!

WE HAVE OUR WONDER GIRL RIGHT HERE.
WHAT DO YOU THINK?

WITH ROLF BRIGGS AROUND, N & B STAFF ARE USED TO THEATRICS.
BUT THIS IS REAL DRAMA.

DID YOU EXPECT ME NOT TO GO WITH HIM, CAL?
HE WAS UPSET.

WE'RE DISCUSSING YOUR STROKE OF GENIUS, NOT YOUR FEVERED COUPLINGS.
NOBODY GASPS, BUT THEY HOLD THEIR BREATH.

YOU ARE REALLY PUSHING IT.
SEEMS TO ME JOSH DID THE PUSHING.

CAL, AS OF NOW, YOU ARE FIRED!

I QUIT!!

CAL?
WHAT? THERE BEEN A TERROR ATTACK?
WHAT?

STOP, LET ME FIX YOU.
I RESIGN.
HUH? WHY?!

CREATIVE DIFFERENCES.

WAIT, CAL. LET'S TALK.
C'MON!

WHY? TALKING MEANS NOTHING.
MONEY AND FAME MEAN EVERYTHING.

IS EVERY CREATIVE TYPE A BIPOLAR DRAMA QUEEN?
DOROTHY NOLAN HAS LONG PRACTICE AT LEAVING THE OBVIOUS COMMENT UNSPOKEN.

MARY, IT'S DOROTHY.

COME IN!

BE RIGHT WITH YOU -- POLISHING OFF THIS EMAIL.
TIKA TIKA

I HEARD ABOUT OUR LITTLE LUNCH-TIME SHOW.
OH, RIGHT.
I FIRED CAL.

WELL, I GATHER IT WAS MUTUAL.
I SUPPOSE. CAL HAS MADE IT CLEAR HE NO LONGER WANTS TO WORK WITH ME.
I GAVE HIM HIS WISH.
MARY...

THERE ARE MANY MANAGEMENT PROBLEMS AT A CREATIVE FIRM LIKE THIS.
WORKPLACE CRUSHES CAN BE DEALT WITH. I CAN HELP YOU WITH THAT.
WORKPL--
OH, DON'T TELL ME YOU DON'T SEE CAL IS SMITTEN.

IN ANY EVENT, CREATIVE PEOPLE SOMETIMES HAVE LESS SELF-CONTROL, OR EVEN AWARENESS OF HOW THEY'RE PERCEIVED.
I'M NOT SAYING THEY DESERVE LICENSE TO BE BIG BABIES...

...BUT YOU CAN OFTEN HEAD OFF THE UNFORGIVABLE.
THESE PEOPLE SPEND A LOT OF TIME IN THEIR OWN HEADS...
...JUDGING WHETHER TWO LINES SHOULD BE CLOSER TOGETHER, OR A DARKER COLOR...AND EXULTING WHEN IT TURNS OUT THEY'RE RIGHT.

AND GOD BLESS 'EM, SOMETIMES THEY CREATE THINGS OF GREAT BEAUTY AND UTILITY.
AS YOU DID, THOUGH THAT'S LOOKING LIKE IT WAS A FLUKE.
IT STINGS, EVEN THOUGH SHE'S LONG KNOWN THIS.

BUT CREATING THE CONDITIONS FOR THEM TO DO WHAT THEY DO...
...THE SAFETY, THE DISCIPLINE, THE CASH FLOW, THE COMITY...
...*THAT* IS DIFFICULT AND JUST AS VALUABLE.

AND IT'S WHAT YOU HAVE AN APTITUDE FOR, I'VE NOTICED.

SURE, THEY'RE CHILDREN, OFTEN.
ESPECIALLY ABOUT MONEY!
BUT WHEN THEY'RE PLAYING IN THEIR IMAGINARY WORLD WITH SYMBOLS AND PICTURES AND SHAPES, THEY *HAVE* TO BE.
NOW LET'S TALK ABOUT WHAT TO DO IF CAL HITS REALITY AND ASKS TO RETURN.

BACK TO MY COFFEE-TABLE BOOK?
I'LL NEED TO REVIVE MY ACCOUNTS.
I WONDER IF TACO HEAVEN AL CAN FORGIVE ME.
JESUS, I CAN BE SUCH A DICK SOMETIMES.

MAN, IT WAS SO GOOD TO BE PART OF SOMETHING BIG.
IT WOULD -- IT'D BE SWEET REVENGE TO EDGE OUT N & B WITH THE CITY.
BUT THAT DAMN MAGIC MARK!

IT'S INVULNERABLE!

345 MILES OF AQUEDUCTS SERVE THE CITY.
MOST ARE AGED AND LEAKING.
NEW YORK CITY
DEPARTMENT OF ENVIRONMENTAL PROTECTION
LOOK THERE, ON THE RIGHT.

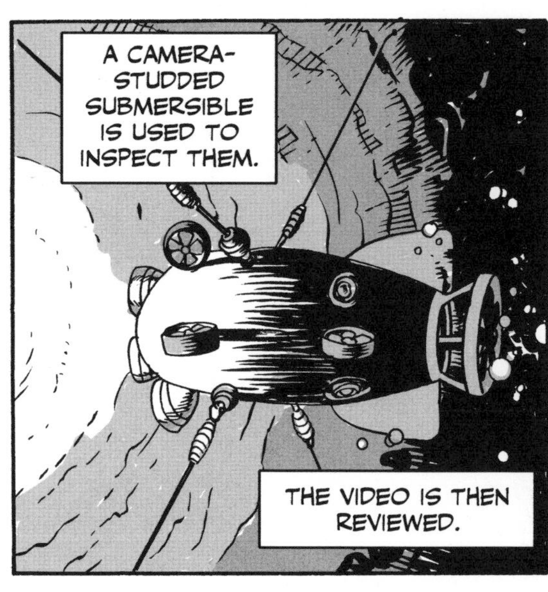
A CAMERA-STUDDED SUBMERSIBLE IS USED TO INSPECT THEM.
THE VIDEO IS THEN REVIEWED.

MY GOD, IT'S TWICE AS BAD AS LAST TIME.
THAT'S IT. SOON IT'LL BE CATASTROPHIC.
WHAT'RE WE LOOKING AT?

DELEWARE AQUEDUCT, MILE 36.
RIGHT WHERE THE SWAMP HAS GROWN UP.
TIME TO PULL THE TRIGGER.
WELL, THEY KNEW THIS WAS COMING.

VOLUNTARY WATER RATIONING GOES INTO EFFECT TODAY, AS AN INTENSIVE REPAIR EFFORT GETS UNDERWAY.
RESTAURANTS WILL SERVE WATER ONLY BY REQUEST AS A REMINDER. LAWN WATER-ING, STREET CLEANING, AND OTHER WATER ACTIVITIES WILL BE CUT BACK OR CURTAILED.

ESTIMATES VARY ON HOW MUCH NEW YORKERS WILL NEED TO CUT BACK.

BUT THE DELEWARE AQUEDUCT DELIVERS NEARLY ONE HALF OF THE CITY'S WATER.

IT'S GOING TO BE A LONG, DRY SUMMER, ISN'T IT, BILL?
LOOKS LIKE IT.

YOUR MEDIA ITINERARY, MARY.
I FEEL MORE AWKWARD THAN EVER ABOUT ALL THIS ATTENTION.
BUT I GUESS THAT'S THE BUSINES WE'RE IN, ISN'T IT?
THAT'S RIGHT.
BUILDING MOMENTUM AND INEVITABILITY BEFORE THE CITY'S DECISION IS CRUCIAL.
PUTTING YOURSELF OUT THERE IS HOW YOU DO THAT.
NOW, THE UPLOAD.
YOUTUBE, YOU ARE MY WHITE HORSE.
AND I SHALL RIDE YOU IN AND CLAIM MY RIGHTFUL PLACE IN POP CULTURE HISTORY.

YES, AL. I'M SORRY. BUT IF YOU NEED SOME-THING, I'M HERE, IS ALL I'M SAYING.
FINE. YOUR TACOS SUCK, BY THE WAY.

1 Message
NYJT 67 LLC
Select
Back

LOOK, CAL, IT'S JOSH. I NEED TO TALK TO YOU. I--
NO, NOT IN A MESSAGE WE NEED TO TALK. CALL ME.

SORRY, JOSH, NOPE.
NOT INTERESTED.

OH, *HI!!*
WELL, THAT SOUNDS TEMPTING...

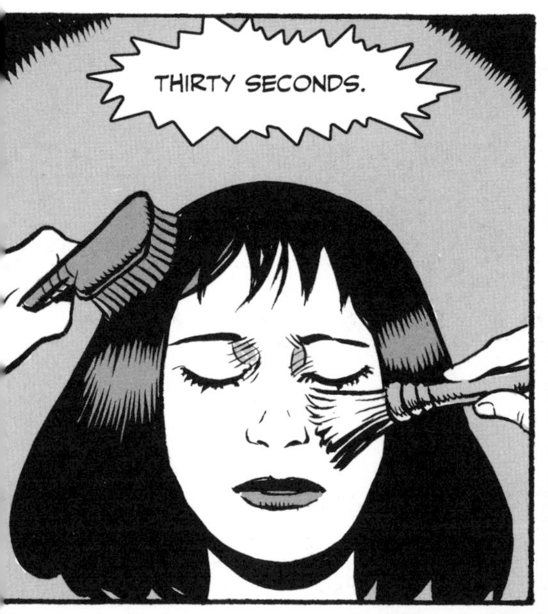
THIRTY SECONDS.

ARE YOU OKAY WITH TAKING CALLS? YOU DON'T HAVE TO, YOU KNOW.
NO, I'M FINE. LET'S.

WE'RE BACK WITH MARY CAPOLAVORO, DESIGNER OF THE SYMBOL THAT'S BEEN EMBRACED BY NEW YORKERS...
...SO MUCH SO THAT IT MAY BE OFFICIALLY ADOPTED AS A LONG-TERM, IF NOT PERMANENT, EMBLEM OF THE CITY.

ANDREW IN WOODSTOCK, NEW YORK, HELLO.
YES, I'M CURIOUS IF MARY IS FAMILIAR WITH THE ZEN WANDERERS ALBUM, "TRASH."
EXIT

OH, I LOVED THAT ALBUM AS A LITTLE GIRL.
MY MOTHER PLAYED IT ALL THE TIME.
WHY DO YOU ASK?

WELL, I'M ANDREW Z. PROBAIN, WHO DESIGNED THE COVER ART FOR THE ALBUM.
I'VE POSTED A 30-SECOND VIDEO ON YOUTUBE THAT SHOWS YOU STOLE THE SYMBOL FROM IT.
THE TITLE IS "MARY RIPPED ME OFF."
I -- I DON'T REMEMBER ANY SYMBOL.

MAYBE IT WAS UNCONSCIOUS.
THE SHOW CAN BROADCAST YOUTUBE CLIPS-- I'VE SEEN IT. HAVE YOUR PRODUCER RE-VIEW IT. IT'S ONLY THIRTY SECONDS, AND I DIDN'T SNEAK IN ANYTHING NAUGHTY.
HAVE MARY WATCH IT ON A MONITOR. I'D LIKE TO SEE HER REACTION.
HE'S RIGHT. AND IT'S DYNAMITE.
OKAY. THIS IS GREAT TV. RUN IT.

I'M GETTING WORD WE'RE GOING TO SHOW YOU THE VIDEO.
I--UM-- OKAY.

I'M ANDREW Z. PROBAIN, AND THIS IS AN ALBUM COVER I DESIGNED 41 YEARS AGO.
TRASH.
ZEN WANDERERS
IT WAS A WRAPAROUND.

WE ZOOM IN ON THE FRONT COVER...
TRASH.
ZEN WANDERERS

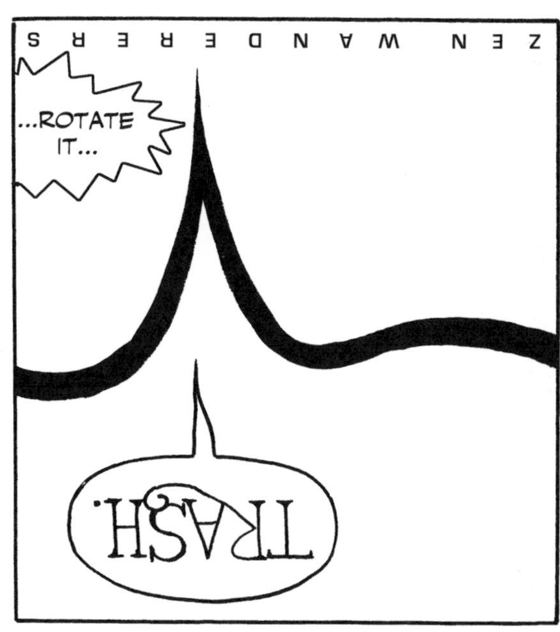
ZEN WANDERERS
...ROTATE IT...
TRASH.

...AND REPLACE THE TEXT.
New York
Our City

MARY, YOU'RE BUSTED.
SECONDS TICK BY.
MARY?

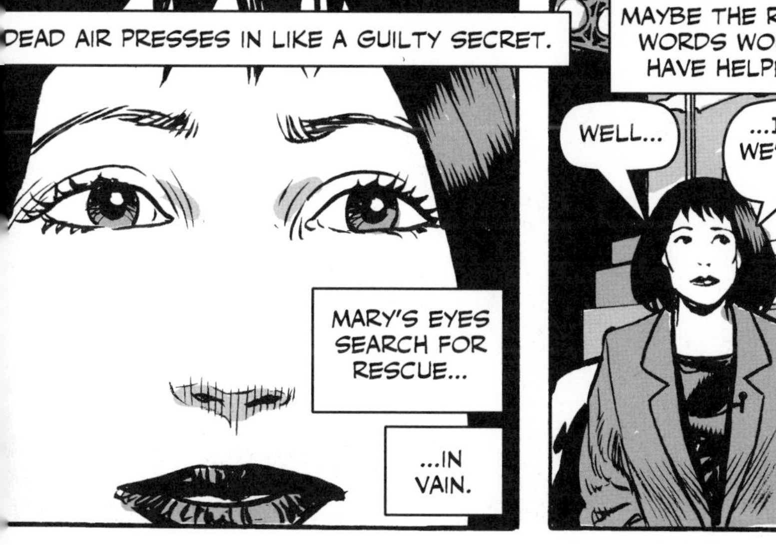
DEAD AIR PRESSES IN LIKE A GUILTY SECRET.
MARY'S EYES SEARCH FOR RESCUE...
...IN VAIN.

MAYBE THE RIGHT WORDS WOULD HAVE HELPED.
BUT THEY DO NOT COME.
WELL...
...I GUESS WE'RE DONE HERE.
AND SO MARY HERSELF BECOMES A VIRAL VIDEO STAR.

NEW YORK POST
Cat Makes more than you p.10
Obama mum on Miley p.16
ART THIEF!
TRASH
YEAH, BABE, I HEARD. I'M SO SORRY, I'VE GOT THIS CELEBRITY CAR RACE IN LONG BEACH.
DAILY NEWS
NYC = TRASH?
Secret message 'Mary's joke'
I SIGNED A CONTRACT!
THIS'LL BLOW OVER. DON'T WORRY.
TONIGHT, A PROFILE OF THE MAN WHO CREATED THE LOOK OF ROCK AND ROLL...
GOD, I HOPE SHE'S OKAY.
BUT THIS DOES GIVE A COMPETITIVE BID A REAL CHANCE.
LET'S GET DESIGNIN'!
...NOT TO MENTION THE ORIGINAL NEW YORK SYMBOL.
HEY, HEY...
MAYBE I DID SOMEHOW REMEMBER IT --
A CLASSY EMBEL-LISHMENT, THAT.
New York
BARF!
THERE'S WORSE. LOOK OVER THERE.

ANYTHING SHOWING PROMISE?
NO.
OR YES. HUNDREDS.
I DON'T KNOW, YOU LOOK AT THEM!

SHE'S DRY AS THE DEAD SEA SCROLLS BEING READ AT AN AA MEETING.
THE MAGIC ISN'T WORKING, YOU'RE SAYING.
I'M SAYING IF SHE'S THE FUKUSHIMA CLEAN-UP CREW, THE SUSHI'S GONNA GLOW IN THE DARK AND HAVE THREE EYES.
IF SHE WERE A BEATLE PETE BES
ALL RIGHT.
LET'S THINK.
WE CAN DOUBLE DOWN ON THE MARK OR HAVE STAFF DO NEW ALTERNA-TIVES.
OR MAYBE BOTH.
BOTH?
DOROTHY NOLAN

FEEL THEM OUT ON THE MARK -- IF IT'S HOPELESS, HIT THEM WITH PLAN B.

BUT I WANT MARY TO BE OUR FACE. SHE'S CHARMED EVERYONE, AND THAT'S HALF THE BATTLE.
I JUST WISH WE COULD GET HER CONFIDENT AGAIN.
SHE AND CAL...
YES, THE SEXUAL TENSION BROUGHT OUT THE BEST IN THEM BOTH.
WANT TO TRY?

NO.
THAT'S NICE, BUT NO.
OH, I HAVE SOMETHING GOING. IN FACT, YOU'LL PROBABLY SEE IT SOON.
NO, IT TAKES ALL MY TIME.
AND THEN SOME.
DAMN, THAT *GLITCH* **AGAIN!**
RESTART!
PIZZA

HOW AM I GOING TO GET THIS PRESENTATION DONE IN TIME?
IF ONLY I COULD HAND OFF SOME OF THE WORK...
...AND GET TECH SUPPORT...
...AND SOME SLEEP...
...I CAN'T NAP UNTIL THE FOOD COMES.

KNOCK KNOCK
705
THE THAI, ALREADY?

JOSH?!
CALVIN RUPP
DESIGN ASSOCIATES
GRAPHIC DESIGN
ADVERTISING
MAY I?
WE HAVE TO TALK.
JUST YOU AND SCREAMY STILL, HUH?
JUST US.
OOK, WALLACE RESEARCHED THIS LEETOLA GUY.
HE'S PRETTY SKETCHY.
HE'S BEEN INVESTIGATED A NUMBER OF TIMES, THOUGH NEVER INDICTED...
...EXCEPT FOR TRANSPORTING EXOTIC ANIMALS ILLEGALLY, WEIRDLY ENOUGH.
PAID A FINE FOR THAT.

ANYWAY, IF THIS DEAL WENT SOUR, I COULD'VE BEEN IN COURT FOR *YEARS.*
EVEN BEING IGNORANT OF WHATEVER THE SCAM WAS, I KNOW I'M A FAT TARGET.
AND THE LAW AT THAT LEVEL IS JUST A KNIFE FIGHT.

YOU SAVED MY ASS, MAN.
YOU AND YOUR INSTINCTS.

I'M SO SORRY.
APOLOGY ACCEPTED.

HOW, UH, IS MARY DOING?
AWFUL. PANICKED. AS YOU MIGHT GUESS.
IT'S ALL CRASHING DOWN, WITH MORE TO COME.
HOW'S THAT?

PROMISE ME, CAL, YOU WON'T GO TO HER WITH THIS.
IT'S SOMETHING I HAVE TO DO MYSELF.
PROMISE!
OKAY...

I SHOULDN'T EVEN SAY ANY MORE, BUT...
...I DON'T THINK SHE AND I ARE IN IT FOR THE LONG HAUL.
THERE, NOW, YOU PROMISED.
I'LL KEEP IT.

KNOCK KNOCK
409
THAI EXPRESS!
I SHOULD GO.

YES, MS. NOLAN. I'VE CHANGED MY MIND.
I'D LIKE TO HELP YOU OUT. I HAVE A PRESENTATION HALF DONE, IN FACT.
WAIT, I HAVE SOME CONDITIONS...

MR. RUPP! GOOD TO SEE YOU BACK.
THANKS, MOIRA.

IT STRIKES HIM: WHY DIDN'T HE PREPARE FOR THIS?
-:- AHEM -:-
WHY DIDN'T HE COMPOSE HEALING, BEAUTIFUL WORDS?
OR BRING A PEACE OFFERING?

WHY COULD HE NOT ANTICIPATE THIS MOMENT?
FORTUNATEL SOMEONE DID.

THE GESTURE IS SIMPLE.

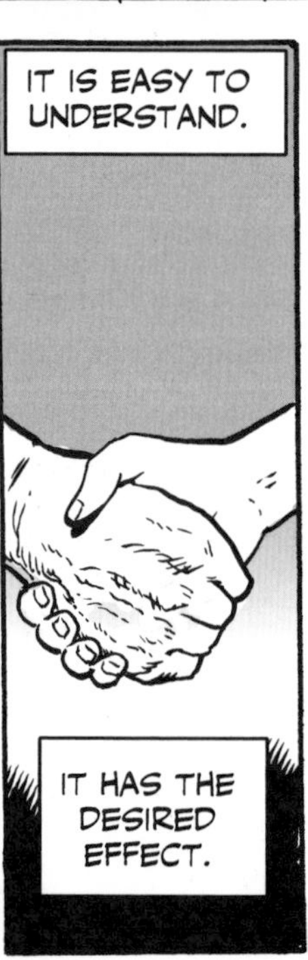
IT IS EASY TO UNDERSTAND.
IT HAS THE DESIRED EFFECT.

THANK YOU.
I'M SO SORRY.
THE GOOD NEWS IS, WE HAVE A JOB TO DO.
LET'S GET STARTED!
SOMETIMES, IT'S JUST THAT EASY.

AND HARD, TOO.
A TREMENDOUS AMOUNT OF WORK MUST BE DONE IN A SHORT TIME.
BUT TASKS ARE DOLED OUT TO OTHERS, AND CRITICAL PATHS IDENTIFIED...
I'LL HAVE CATHERINE DO THAT. YOU MOVE ON TO THE ANIMATION.
...AND FOR THE FIRST TIME IN A WHILE, CAL KNOWS JUST WHAT TO DO NEXT, EVERY DAY.
IT'S CLARIFYING. EXHILARATING, EVEN.
AND SOMEHOW, THEY ARE READY IN TIME FOR THE PRESENTATION.
YEAH, I HAD AN IDEA FOR THAT.

AT CITY HALL.
YOU TWO SET?
DON'T CHOKE ON THIS PRESENTATION OR ANYTHING!
I JUST WISH WE DIDN'T HAVE TO DO THIS *HERE.* THINGS GO WRONG.
nolan & briggs
PROJECTOR WORKING?
WE DID FOUR RUN-THROUGHS.
nolan & briggs
AND WE HAVE A SPARE.

BEFORE WE GET STARTED, WE'D BEST ACKNOWLEDGE THE ELEPHANT IN THE ROOM.
THE MARK HAS HAD A RUN OF BAD PUBLICITY THESE PAST WEEKS.

THIS ISN'T NECESSARILY FATAL, AND WE HAVE A FULL PRO-GRAM FOR ITS IMPLEMENTATION TO SHOW YOU.
BUT WE ALSO HAVE AN ALTERNATIVE.
AT NOLAN & BRIGGS WE PRIDE OURSELVES ON BEING NIMBLE AND REALISTIC.

ONE MOMENT.
I SUGGEST WE NOT WASTE TIME WITH THIS OBIVOUS CATASTROPHE OUT OF MERE POLITENESS!
I NEVER THOUGHT IT WAS PARTICULARLY ENCHANTING EVEN AT ITS HEIGHT OF EXPOSURE.

<MY COLON NO LIKEE.>
< WAIT UNTIL THE LIGHTS ARE DOWN.>

I'M AFRAID THE LEGAL EXPOSURE SETTLES THE ISSUE.
AND THAT ASIDE, NO ONE PROFITS BY ASSOCIATING THE CITY WITH THE WORD "TRASH."
NOR WITH A PROG-ROCK BAND THAT SINGS ABOUT SUICIDE AND NUCLEAR WAR.
I NEVER SAW WHAT WAS SO SPECIAL ABOUT IT, MYSELF.
nolan & briggs

GOOD!
EVERYTHING THAT HELPS THE PROCESS ALONG IS A POSITIVE.
MARY, CAL, PLEASE PROCEED.

I'LL BE CO-PRESENTING WITH CAL RUPP, OUR LEAD DESIGNER ON THIS PROJECT.
IT WAS CAL WHO CAME UP WITH THIS NEW APPROACH AND DID THE LION'S SHARE OF THE EXECUTION.
HI.

ONE OF THE GUIDANCE OBJECTIVES PROVIDED BY THE CITY TOURISM BOARD WAS APPEAL TO YOUNG PEOPLE.
AND WE TOOK THIS TO HEART.
AND THIS BIT OF STROKING SEEMS TO BRING WARMTH TO THE NYCTB CHAIR'S EYES.

THE CITY'S GLEAMING MODERNITY SPEAKS FOR ITSELF.
BUT IT ALSO HAS ITS HERITAGE -- AND IN THAT A SORT OF ROMANCE.
QUIETLY, ROLF TAKES THIS MOMENT TO BEGIN HIS QUEST FOR GASTRIC RELIEF.

AS MARY'S CONSIDERED WORDS PREPARE THE WAY FOR THE BIG REVEAL, ROLF'S CAREFUL STEPS BRING HIM ACROSS THE DARK ROOM.

...AND THE RESULT, THEN, IS...
KRAASH!
BZZZZT
TINKLE!

WELL, WE'RE ALL REALLY AWAKE, NOW! I KNOW *I* AM.
WHILE CAL SETS UP THE OTHER PROJECTOR, LET ME TELL YOU A STORY.
"PREPARE FOR UN-EXPECTED GLITCHES," DOROTHY HAD TOLD HER..

IT'S NOT A BAD ANEC-DOTE...ABOUT THE WHIRL-WIND AROUND THE MARK, AND MARY'S MEDIA NAIVETE.
IT'S SELF-DEPRECATING AND GETS A LAUGH.
...AND WE'RE READY. CAL?

"AS YOU SEE, IT'S BASED ON THE NEW, RETRO LAMP POSTS."
"WITH A MAN AND A WOMAN BENEATH, LOOKING AT EACH OTHER BUT NOT TOUCHING."
"THAT'S DELIBERATE. THIS WAY, WE WONDER -- HAVE THEY JUST MET? OR IS IT A RENDEZVOUS? WE MAKE UP OUR OWN STORY."
New York.
Our city.
"YES, WE KNOW IT'LL BE PARODIED. THE CITY ITSELF CAN SWITCH OUT WHO'S STANDING THERE..."
"...TIE IT TO CURRENT EVENTS, FADS, FASHIONS. IT'S FLEXIBLE."
"BUT ONE THING'S FOR CERTAIN..."

"EVERY TOURIST COUPLE WILL POSE UNDER ONE..."
"...FOR THE ESSENTIAL SOUVENIR PHOTO."

"AND THERE WILL BE A THOUSAND OPPORTUNITIES TO DO SO ACROSS THE CITY."

"WHICH ARE WAITING IN A WAREHOUSE READY TO BE INSTALLED."

"AND THERE ARE NO ISSUES OF AUTHORSHIP."
"THE CITY ITSELF COMMISSIONED THE DESIGN IN 1902..."

"...FROM SCULPTOR MORTIMER HARSHAW EVERETT, WHO STUDIED WITH, THEN BITTERLY SPLIT FROM, FREDERIC BARTHOLDI."

"EVERETT WOULD SMILE TO SEE THAT FOR A MOMENT, HE IS UPSTAGING THE MAKER OF THE STATUE OF LIBERTY."
"HE WED A VANDERBILT AND, SADLY, THEY BOTH WENT DOWN WITH THE *LUSITANIA*."

CHILDLESS, I MIGHT ADD.
A MURMUR OF LEGAL RELIEF FOLLOWS.
MARY FIGHTS A SMILE.
CAL WILL TAKE YOU THROUGH SOME OF THE IMPLE- MENTATION.
HERE WE HAVE A...

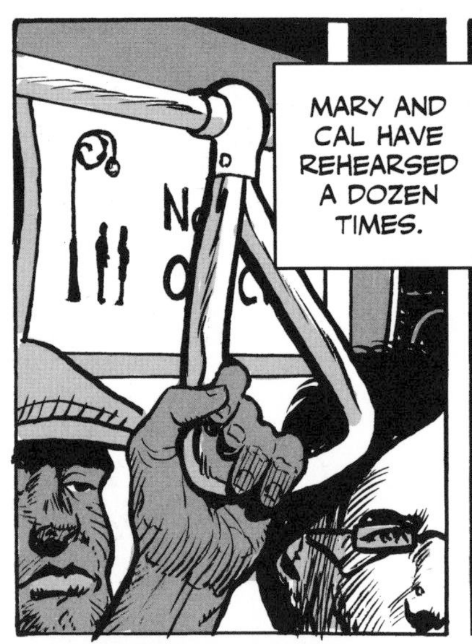
MARY AND CAL HAVE REHEARSED A DOZEN TIMES.

CAL EXPLAINS HIS THINKING FOR EACH CHOICE HE'S MADE.

IT HAS THE INHERENT INTEREST OF ANSWERING THE EVERGREEN QUESTION: "WHY?"

NORMAN ROCKWELL OBSERVED, "GENIUS IS THE CAPACITY TO TAKE INFINITE PAINS."
N.Y.C.
DEPARTMENT OF SANITATION

New York
Our City.

AS THE PAINS CAL AND THE TEAM HAVE TAKEN BECOME EVIDENT, THE CAMPAIGN SEEMS *REAL.*
IT'S AS IF IT'S ALREADY TAKEN PLACE.

STILL AS THE PRESENTATIOIN ENDS...
...INEVITABLE TENSION GROWS.

I HAVEN'T SEEN THAT MUCH CRAP SINCE THE ELEPHANT PARADE!
WONDER IF I COULD USE THAT ON THIS CROWD?
BUT BEFORE ANY APT MOMENT PRESENTS ITSELF...
WE'RE SOLD.
IT'S A BRILLIANT SOLUTION.
THAT THE STREETLAMPS HAD SPAWNED WHISPERS OF "THE MAYOR'S FOLLY" WAS A WIND AT THEIR BACKS.
STILL, IT IS A VICTORY, AND A VICTORY MUST BE CELEBRATED.
WE'RE EATIN' HAUTE JAPANESE!
JC38
YOU'LL LIKE THIS PLACE. THE WALLS ARE MADE OUTTA BOOKS.
YOU KNOW "BRUSTROKE" ON HUDSON?
OH, YES. MY BIGGEST TIPPER EVER HAD ME TAKE HIM THERE.
SUBTLE MAN!

KAISEKI MENU FOR EVERYONE!

GIVES ME AN IDEA OF WHAT TO DO WITH ALL MY *COMMUNICATION ARTS* ANNUALS.
COURSE ONE OF TEN IS HERE.

THE MEETING IS RELIVED, AND CONGRATULATIONS REPEATED.
THE FUTURE OF NOLAN & BRIGGS IS PAINTED IN ROSY TINTS.
MARY AND CAL'S POSITIONS THERE ARE IMPLICITLY ASCENDANT.
SOMEHOW IT IRKS CAL.

I THINK I ATE ONE SEA SLUG TOO MANY.
THAT WAS KELP, ROLF DEAR.
WE HAVE AN OFFICE PARTY TO PLAN.
CAN YOU TWO SEE YOURSELVES HOME?

I'M STILL WORKED UP. SEEMS KIND OF ANTI-CLIMACTIC.
I HAVE A SILLY IDEA. I HOPE YOU WON'T THINK I'M STUPID.
OF COURSE NOT.

LET'S GO UP TO THE LAMPPOST.
AND THANK IT.

IT'S AS GOOD AN IDEA AS ANY.
AND, IT REMAINS UNSPOKEN, PERHAPS A CERTAIN MOMENT MIGHT BE *RELEIVED...*
Exit
...AND EVEN NUDGED TOWARD A *FULFILLMENT.*

WAIT-- THIS ISN'T THE BLOCK.
YOU'RE RIGHT. IT'S UPTOWN.
Cent
1 9

LOOK, WE'RE NEAR THE FOUNTAIN.
NOT THAT I GOT MY WISH.
WHAT WAS IT?

ABOUT JOSH.
TRUE LOVE.
GIRL STUFF.

I THOUGHT HE WAS ALL OVER YOU.
HE WAS, FOR A WHILE.
HE HASN'T TOUCHED ME SINCE...THAT DINNER WITH MAGDA.
I CAN TELL HE'S IN SOME SORT OF TURMOIL.

I GUESS HE SAID SOMETHING ALONG THOSE LINES.
WHEN?!
BEFORE I CAME BACK.
AT MY PLACE.

W-WHAT WAS HE DOING THERE?
THAT TIME, APOLOGIZING.
EARLIER -- KINDA WEIRD, THIS -- HE GAVE THE PLACE AN IKEA MAKEOVER.
BEHIND MY BACK.

WHAT --?! HE BOUGHT *ME* SOME IKEA FURNITURE!
I USED TO THINK HE WAS TRYING TO MESS WITH MY HEAD, WARNING ME OFF YOU, SOMEHOW.
BUT I KIND OF THINK HE LIKES ME.

I KNOW HE DOES.
HE SAID SO.
WITH A LOT OF FEELING.
IN BED.

O-KAY... WHOA.
I KIND OF SUSPECTED, BUT GUYS TRY TO DENY THIS STUFF.
I CAN'T SAY I SAW IT MYSELF.
IT'S FUNNY, MARY. IT'S ALMOST AS IF I GOT *YOUR* WISH WITH *MY* COIN.

YOUR COIN?
FTER THE NVEILING ND SUCH.
I WISHED FOR MY TALENT TO BE RECOGNIZED.

YOU...
THE MARK!

WELL, HOW FAR DOES THIS GO?
ARE YOU ATTRACTED TO JOSH?
BEFORE I ANSWER...
...LET ME CLARIFY ONE THING.
IT'S BREAKING A PROMISE, BUT I THINK IT'S JUSTIFIED.
JOSH DIDN'T SAY HE WAS IN *TURMOIL*...

..HE SAID YOU ND HE WEREN'T OING TO BE IN FOR THE LONG HAUL.
OH.

YOU DON'T SEEM CRUSHED.
NO.

HE DOESN'T ANSWER IN WORDS.

IT'S A KISS.

IT'S *THE* KISS.
SOMETHING BEGINS.

AS A FOUNTAIN'S WATER FLOWS, UNMEASURED, SO DOES TIME, IN A HAZE OF GIDDY WONDER.
8670
DEPARTMENT OF EVIRONMENTAL PROTECTION OFFICIALS SAY AQUEDUCT REPAIRS ARE COMPLETE.
WHAT YESTERDAY WERE RESPECTED WORKPLACE BOUNDARIES ARE NOW CAST AWAY WITH THE EASE OF SILK SLIPPING OFF SKIN.
I'VE WANTED THIS SO LONG...
ME, TOO, SINCE THAT NIGHT, WALKING.
BOTH THE HARLEM MEER AND THE JACQUELINE KENNEDY ONASSIS RESERVIOR IN CENTRAL PARK ARE EXPECTED TO REACH NORMAL LEVELS WITHIN TWO WEEKS.
OTHER PARK WATER USES ARE BEING RESTORED AS WELL.
OR BEFORE.
I DON'T KNOW...
IN OTHER NEWS, NEW YORK WILL BE GETTING A NEW LOOK IN ITS STREET LIGHTING...
...OR, RATHER, AN OLD LOOK, AS INSTALLATION RESUMES OF...
BZZZT!
DAMN.

MARY, IT'S JOSH.

I THOUGHT YOU WERE IN CALIFORNIA!
I'M BACK. WE NEED TO TALK.
LET HIM UP.
CAL, PLEASE STAY IN THE BEDROOM.
IT'S NOT THE RIGHT WAY, WE DON'T KNOW...
WE KNOW IT'S OVER.

YES, IT'S OVER, BUT JOSH IS A PROUD MAN.
AND HE'S A PRO ATHLETE, FOR GOD'S SAKE!!
DO IT FOR ME -- OH, I'D DIE IF HE HURT YOU!
BE REALISTIC!
OH, ALL RIGHT.

I'LL GET YOU WHEN THE COAST IS CLEAR.
BING BONG
SUPER.
COMING!

HE HEARS VOICES, BUT NOT THE WORDS.
MADDENING.
EVERY INSTINCT TELLS HIM TO GO OUT AND CLAIM WHAT IS HIS.

AND INSTINCT WINS.
NO--!

EYES LOCK.

TIME SLOWS.

A REACTION FORMS.

HA HA HA HA
HA
HEE
HEE
HA
HA
OH GOD OH GOD

I FAIL TO SEE THE LEVITY.
I'M SORRY --
HEE HEE
IT'S JUST...

IT'S JUST THAT I'VE BEEN DREADING THIS SO MUCH.
AND THIS MAKES IT EASIER.

IN FACT, I CAN SPEED THINGS UP, NOW.
IT'S ME. YOU STILL THERE?
YEP.
COME UP.

I'VE..
...BEEN GOING THROUGH SOME THINGS.
JETS
CAL, SORRY IF I FREAKED YOU OUT.
SOMETHING STRONG GOT AHOLD OF ME AND WOKE UP SOMETHING I'D TRIED TO LEAVE BEHIND.

MARY, YOU'RE INCREDIBLE, AND IN THE WAY THAT PEOPLE LEAN ONE WAY OR THE OTHER, I THOUGHT I WAS OKAY AT 60-40.
BUT I WASN'T. I'M NOT. I'M 80-20.
OR MAYBE 90-10.
I'M NOT THAT SMART BUT I'M SMART ENOUGH TO KNOW THIS DOESN'T LAST LONG. ONE DAY I'LL COME OUT AND STRIKE A BLOW FOR TOLERANCE.
ALL THAT.
BUT IT'S A BIG DEAL IN MY BUSINESS.
MAYBE NOT A CAREER-ENDER.
ENDORSEMENT KILLER, PROBABLY.
TEAM COHESION KILLER, FOR SURE.
SPEND A DAY IN A LOCKER ROOM AND YOU'LL KNOW I'M RIGHT.
MAYBE I'M A COWARD FOR NOT WANTING THE END THE CAROUSEL RIDE EARLY.
BUT I DON'T.
THE RIDE'S PRETTY GOOD.
FEW PEOPLE IN LIFE GET IT, EVER.

SO MY LIFE IS IN YOUR HANDS.
IF YOU'RE ANGRY, YOU'RE ENTITLED.
I LIED--MAYBE THE BIGGEST LIE ONE PERSON CAN TELL ANOTHER.
BUT IT'S ONLY A HALF-LIE.
I LOVE YOUR GOODNESS, YOUR GENTLENESS--YOU'RE BEAUTIFUL IN EVERY WAY.
YOU'RE ALL A MAN COULD WANT IN A WOMAN.
I'M JUST NOT THAT KIND OF MAN.

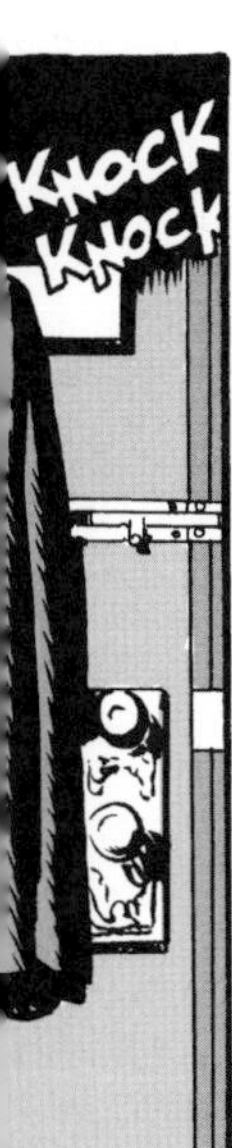
KNOCK
KNOCK

HANG ON!

YOU REMEMBER WALLACE.
SINCE RACING DAY, IN CASE YOU WERE WONDERING.
HI.
HOW, UH, DID THIS GO?

I -- I'M NOT SURE WHAT TO SAY.

BUT SHE REMEMBERS A RECENT, WORDLESSLY ELOQUENT ANSWER.
THIS TIME, IT SPEAKS TO ALL IN THE ROOM.
"IT'S OKAY. WE'RE IN LOVE. NO HARM DONE HERE."

"WHO FELT WHAT, AND WHEN?" IT'S ENDLESSLY FASCINATING.
THEY LAUGH. THEY CHOKE UP. THEY SEE THROUGH NEW EYES.
THE BEER IS COLD. THE ACCEPTANCE, THE CUDDLING, ARE DELICIOUS.

MARY SAYS IT:
"I COULDN'T HAVE WISHED FOR A BETTER ENDING."

IN A LEARJET...
...A DIAMOND NECKLACE...
...FALLS.
OH!

HERE, LET ME.
LET ME LOOK AT IT IN MY COMPACT MIRROR.

OH NO! DID I LEAVE MY PURSE IN MONTREAL?
LET ME SEE.

YES, IN THE LIMOUSINE.
BUT THEY'LL SHIP IT -- IT'LL BE IN ST. MARTIN TOMORROW.

WILL MY PASSPORT BE A PROBLEM?
NOT UNLESS WE'RE REGISTERING TO MARRY.

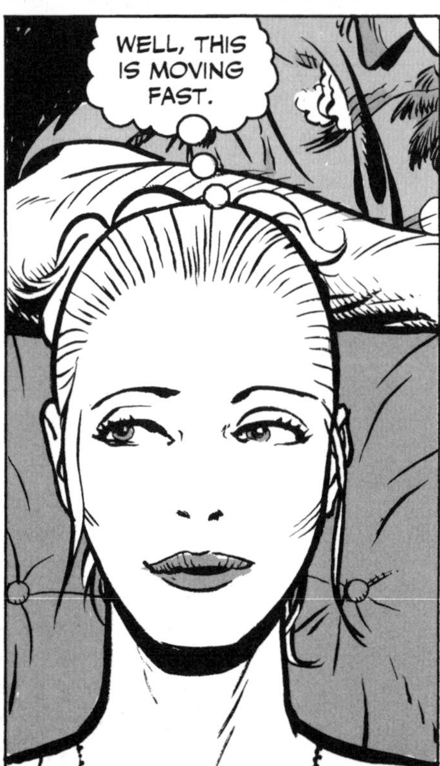
WELL, THIS IS MOVING FAST.

TWO
EARS
ATER
DO YOU REALLY THINK IT NEEDS THE NUMBERS, CAL?
20 flights daily to the Caribbean
AIR AZUL

TOO OBVIOUS OR TOO SUBTLE.
THAT'S THE SALES POINT THEY WANTED.
LET ME SHOW IT AROUND FOR REACTIONS BOTH WAYS.
OH, MS. RUPP...

HERE'S THE PLAN FOR THE OFFICE DAY-CARE.
NOT AS EXPENSIVE AS WE FEARED.
ALSO, YOUR TWO O'CLOCK IS HERE.

OH, THE RE-BRANDING.
THEY WANT CAL TO DO FOR THEM WHAT HE DID FOR THE CITY.
YOU UP FOR IT, HON?

"I DON'T KNOW. CAN'T GUARANTEE A TOUCHDOWN EVERY TIME."
Rupp & Rupp
"CAL, DEAR, I'LL TELL THEM TOUCHDOWNS ARE YOUR SPECIALTY."

LIFE GOES ON.
NEW YORKERS STRIVE, HOPE, YEARN.
THEY HOLD ON TO GOOD HABITS. SOMETIMES.
AND THEY WISH.

I WISH I COULD DO SOMETHING TO MAKE MYSELF RICH AND FAMOUS.

I WISH THAT I BECOME PREGNANT.
THE END

MIKE RICHARDSON is best known as the publisher, president, and founder of Dark Horse Comics and as a film and television producer at Dark Horse Entertainment. Mike has also written a number of acclaimed comics series and original graphic novels, including *47 Ronin* (nominated for a 2014 Eisner Award for Best Limited Series), *Father's Day*, and *Echoes*. In addition, Mike has created an arsenal of unforgettable characters such as the Mask, Timecop, X, and the Atomic Legion. An avid collector and longtime owner of the Things From Another World comics-shop chain, Mike's encyclopedic knowledge of comics and pop-culture history are featured in his contributions to the books *Comics Between the Panels* and *Blast Off!: Rockets, Robots, Ray Guns, and Rarities from the Golden Age of Space Toys*.

PAUL CHADWICK is the creator of *Concrete*, the acclaimed series about a man whose mind is trapped inside a hulking alien body. Paul and *Concrete* have claimed numerous awards, including seven Eisners, two Harveys, and a Reuben Award from the National Cartoonist Society. Paul is also the architect of *The World Below*, a fascinating tale of explorers in a bizarre land beneath Washington state. Paul has used the skills he honed at Art Center College of Design to create storyboards, movie advertising, book and magazine illustration, and has drawn comics for Marvel, DC, Dark Horse, and others. Paul also spent three years writing for *The Matrix Online*, expanding the world created in the hit film trilogy. Prior to *Best Wishes*, Paul's most recent work in comics was collaborating with Harlan Ellison on the graphic novel *7 Against Chaos*.

THE ATOMIC LEGION
With Bruce Zick
978-1-61655-312-8 | $29.99

47 RONIN
With Stan Sakai
978-1-59582-954-2 | $19.99

THE SECRET
With Jason Shawn Alexander
978-1-59307-821-8 | $12.99

LIVING WITH THE DEAD: A ZOMBIE BROMANCE Second Edition
With Ben Stenbeck and Richard Corben
978-1-50670-062-5 | $9.99

CUT
With Todd Herman and Mike Mignola
978-1-59307-845-4 | $9.99

CRAVAN: MYSTERY MAN OF THE TWENTIETH CENTURY
With Rick Geary
978-1-59307-291-9 | $14.99

WALT DISNEY'S RETURN OF THE GREMLINS
With Dean Yeagle
978-1-61655-669-3 | $19.99

FATHER'S DAY
With Gabriel Guzman
978-1-61655-579-5 | $14.99

ECHOES
With Gabriel Guzman
978-1-50670-123-3 | $14.99

BEST WISHES
With Paul Chadwick
978-1-50670-374-9 | $19.99